Guide to Creating a Kemetic Marriage Contract

By
Muata Ashby and Dja Ashby

Sema Institute of Yoga
P. O. Box 570459
Miami, Florida, 33257
(305) 378-6253 Fax: (305) 378-6253

©2017 By Sema Institute of Yoga

All rights reserved. No part of this book may be used or reproduced in any manner whatsoever without written permission (address above) except in the case of brief quotations embodied in critical articles and reviews. All inquiries may be addressed to the address above.

The author is available for group lectures. For further information contact the publisher.

Guide to Creating a Kemetic Marriage Contract by Muata Ashby and Karen Dja Ashby
ISBN: 1-884564-82-8

This manual is based on the Lecture series Kemetic Marriage and Relationships 2011 by Sebai Dr. Muata Ashby

Based on the books:

INTRODUCTION TO MAAT PHILOSOPHY: Spiritual Enlightenment Through the Path of Virtue

SACRED SEXUALITY: ANCIENT EGYPTIAN TANTRA YOGA: The Art of Sex Sublimation and Universal Consciousness

TABLE OF CONTENTS

Contents

Introduction: Kemetic Culture and Philosophy 10
   Ancient Egyptian Wisdom Foundations for Kemetic Relationships Philosophy 10
   HOW DID MARRIAGE COME TO BE THOUGHT OF AS IT IS TODAY? 14
   MARRIAGE IN ANCIENT EGYPT 15
Chapter 1: The Process of Constructing a Kemetic Marital Agreement (Kemetic Marriage Contract) 28
   Non-negotiable Maatian principles: 30
   Non-negotiable personal principles: 32
   Honoring Self and Exercising Freedom while Honoring the Feelings of the Other Person and Handling Conflict 34
      Handling conflicts constructively 35
   Handling Minor infractions of the agreement 39
   Handling Major infractions of the agreement 39
   DIVORCE: 39
   STEPS FOR ARRIVING AT A MARITAL AGREEMENT 39
CHAPTER 2: GUIDING QUESTIONS TO HELP YOU WORK THROUGH THE ISSUES AND ARRIVING AT A FINAL AGREEMENT 43
CHAPTER 3: INSTRUCTIONS FOR DEVELOPING YOUR PROPOSALS THAT WILL BE REFLECTED UPON FIRST & THEN HOW TO DISCUSS THEM WITH YOUR PROSPECTIVE PARTNER AND THEN ARRIVE AT THE FINAL AGREEMENT WITH YOUR PARTNER 49
   Note on the proposals: 51
CHAPTER 4: WORKSHEETS to develop the principles that will go into the contract .. 52
   WORKSHEET FOR PRINCIPLE: Honoring yourself and your partner 53
   WORKSHEET FOR PRINCIPLE: Religion 55
   WORKSHEET FOR PRINCIPLE: Finances 57
   WORKSHEET FOR PRINCIPLE: Sex 59
   WORKSHEET FOR PRINCIPLE: Progeny 61
   WORKSHEET FOR PRINCIPLE: Health 63
   WORKSHEET FOR PRINCIPLE: Chores and Family responsibilities 65
   WORKSHEET FOR PRINCIPLE: Divorce 67
   WORKSHEET FOR PRINCIPLE: Death 69
   WORKSHEET FOR PRINCIPLE: Other_____ 71
   WORKSHEET FOR PRINCIPLE: Other_____ 73

CHAPTER 5: PUTTING THE FINAL STATEMENTS INTO THE FINAL MARITAL AGREEMENT/CONTRACT DOCUMENT 75
    Samples Kemetic Marriage Contracts 75
    General Framework of Agreement: 77
    CLAUSES CREATED BY PATNER #1 77
    Partner #1- Non-Negotiable Principles 77
    Partner #1- Principles To Honor Partner #1's Soul: 78
    Partner #1's Principles to Honor Partner #2's Soul: 78
    CLAUSES CREATED BY PATNER #2 79
    Partner #2's Non – Negotiable Principles 79
    Partner #2's Principles To Honor Partner #2's Soul 80
    Partner #2's Principles To Honor Partner #1's Soul 80
    Partner #1 and Partner #2 Mutual Agreements 80
INDEX 82
Other Books From C M Books 86

Bio for Dr. Muata Ashby

Dr. Muata Ashby began studies in the area of religion and philosophy and achieved a doctorate degree in these areas while at the same time he began to collect his research into what would later become several books on the subject of the African History, religion and ethics, world mythology, origins of Yoga Philosophy and practice in ancient Africa (Ancient Egypt/Nubia) and also the origins of Christianity in Ancient Egypt. This was the catalyst for a successful book series on the subject called "Egyptian Yoga" begun in 1994. He has extensively studied mystical religious traditions from around the world and is an accomplished lecturer, musician, artist, poet, painter, screenwriter, playwright and author of over 65 books on yoga philosophy, religious philosophy and social philosophy based on ancient African principles. A leading advocate of the concept of the existence of advanced social and religious philosophy in ancient Africa comparable to the Eastern traditions such as Vedanta, Buddhism, Confucianism and Taoism, he has lectured and written extensively on the correlations of these with ancient African religion and philosophy.

Muata Abhaya Ashby holds a Doctor of Divinity Degree from the American Institute of Holistic Theology and a Masters degree in Liberal Arts and Religious Studies from Thomas Edison State College. He has performed extensive researched Ancient Egyptian philosophy and social order as well as Maat philosophy, the ethical foundation of Ancient Egyptian society.

Dr. Ashby has been an independent researcher and practitioner of Egyptian Yoga, Indian Yoga, Chinese Yoga, Buddhism and mystical psychology as well as Christian Mysticism. Dr. Ashby has engaged in Post Graduate research in advanced Jnana, Bhakti and Kundalini Yogas at the Yoga Research Foundation.

Since 1999 he has researched Ancient Egyptian musical theory and created a series of musical compositions which explore this unique area of music from ancient Africa and its connection to world music. Dr. Ashby has lectured around the United States of America, Europe and Africa.

In recent years he has researched the world economy in the last 300 years, focusing on the United States of America and western culture in general. He is also a Teacher of Yoga Philosophy and Discipline. Dr. Ashby is an adjunct professor at the American Institute of Holistic Theology and worked as an adjunct professor at the Florida International University.

In the last two years with the reorganization of the Kemet University and the introduction of the Egyptian Mystery School along with a tailored learning system making use of the Ancient Egyptian Temple teaching elements along with modern technologies Dr. Ashby has engendered a new phase of dissemination of the teachings introducing a new dynamism to the books as well as the live lectures given over the last 25 years.

Currently he is focusing on projects related to the temples of Aset and of Asar, doing detailed photographic work and presenting new original translations of the related hieroglyphic scriptures while teaching those through the Kemet University Egyptian Mystery School online and through in person seminars and conferences.

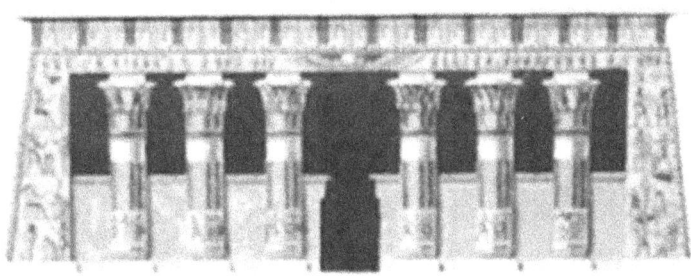

Dr. Muata Ashby began to function in the capacity of *Sebai* or Spiritual Preceptor of Shetaut Neter, Ancient Egyptian Religion [Including the Temple of Aset] and also as Ethics Philosopher and Religious Studies instructor. When operating as a professor in an academic setting he is addressed as Dr. Ashby. When operating in the capacity of temple priest he is addressed as Sebai MAA.

Through his studies of the teachings of the great philosophers of the world and meeting with and studying under spiritual masters and having practiced advanced meditative disciplines, Dr. Ashby began to function in the capacity of Sebai or Spiritual Preceptor of Shetaut Neter, Ancient Egyptian Religion and also as Ethics Philosopher and Religious Studies instructor. Thus his title is Sebai and the acronym of his Kemetic and western names is MAA. He believes that it is important to understand all religious teachings in the context of human historical, cultural and social development in order to promote greater understanding and the advancement of humanity.

Bio: Dr. Dja Ashby

Dr. Dja Ashby, also called Seba Dja was born in Guyana, South America, as Karen Clarke. She was born to a heritage including African, Native American and European cultures. In 1974 her family moved to the United States.

Dr. Dja Ashby is the co-founder of the Sema Institute of Yoga which is a non-profit organization established by her and her spiritual partner, Dr. Muata Ashby, author of over 60 books on the subject of the origins of Yoga Philosophy and practice in ancient Africa (Kamit - Ancient Egypt) and also the origins of Christian Mysticism in Ancient Egypt.

The Sema Institute is dedicated to spreading the wisdom of Ancient African Kamitan Yoga and the Ancient Egyptian mystical traditions through their books, seminars, online classes, and distance learning courses.

Dr. Dja Ashby and Dr. Muata Ashby have been married for 30 years.

Dr. Dja Ashby is also director of C.M. Book Publishing, a branch of the Sema Institute, which publishes the Egyptian Yoga Book series, and editor of the Egyptian Yoga Book Series.

Dr. Dja Ashby is the author of "De-stressing 101: Tools For Living A Stress Free Life", which teaches how to understand stress and to prevent, stop and counter the effects of stress.

She is also co-author of "Tjef Neteru, Movement of the Gods and Goddesses, The Egyptian Yoga Exercise Workout Book" which details the physical postures and exercises practiced thousands of years ago in Ancient Egypt which are today known as Hatha Yoga in the West. This work is based on the pictures and teachings from the Creation story of Ra, The Osirian Resurrection Myth and the carvings and reliefs from various Temples in Ancient Egypt.

She is also contributing author on "Kemetic Diet, Ancient African Wisdom for Health of Body, Mind and Spirit - The Real "Soul" Food" which presents the concepts and teachings based on the Kemetic (Ancient Egyptian) philosophy of total health of the entire person, that is, health not just of the body, but also health of the mind and soul as well, which gets to the root cause of the dis-ease and eradicates it.

Dr. Dja Ashby is also an independent researcher, practitioner and teacher of Yoga, a Doctor in the Sciences (veterinarian) and a Pastoral Counselor, and has engaged in post-graduate research in advanced Indian Yoga, specifically Jnana, Bhakti, Karma, Raja and Kundalini Yogas

She is a certified Yoga Exercise instructor both in the Kemetic Tjef Neteru Sema Paut (Kamitan Yoga Exercise system) and Indian traditions, and a teacher of health and stress management uses of Yoga for modern society.

Dr. Dja Ashby is a certified and Indian Hatha Yoga Exercise instructor, the Coordinator and Instructor for the Level 1 Teacher Certification Tjef Neteru Sema Training programs, and a teacher of health and stress management applications of the Yoga / Sema Tawi systems for modern society, based on the Kamitan and/or Indian yogic principles.

TEMPLE OF SHETAUT NETER   The Sema Institute   Kemet University

Introduction: Kemetic Culture and Philosophy

Ancient Egyptian Wisdom Foundations for Kemetic Relationships Philosophy

This program was, as I said before, it was instigated by the need to have a clearer understanding of the Kemetic concepts of relationships and marriage, specifically for anyone who wants to enter into marriage now but generally for everyone else especially those who are in a relationship at this time or who are contemplating and desiring to enter into a relationship.

This volume is not and was not intended as a sentimental kind of "how to" manual with instructions on how to make your relationship and or marriage work wonderfully and how you can be great partners and hold hands all the time and walk into the sunset forever and to the end of time, etc. I am being a little sarcastic but you get the point. This is not intended as a "New Age" just believe and everything will be perfect – program since in real life that sells books but does not work in relationships unless people are deluded, in which case why take this course?

This volume is going to be more related to a realistic and philosophical outlook which as some of you, people who have not attended lectures or do not know me from that standpoint or who are coming new or fresh to it may take it in the wrong way. I have given, in the past, some touchy-feely programs as appropriate. What I mean by this term is a program that caters to or emphasizes sentimentalities and feelings, which have their place. I refer you to the lecture that we did six years ago in Atlanta and also we did a previous lecture series, back in the 1990's within the Maat lecture series, there is a section on relationships and marriage also. So, I refer you to those. This present series will emphasize more of the philosophy and wisdom behind the Kemetic Marital Ethics but also the ethical Maatian principles as they are to be applied to other relationships such as with friends, parents and children, nature, animals, other countries, etc.. The following principles will act as guides for our study of Kemetic Relationships.

THE KEMETIC PRINCIPLES OF MARRIAGE

- Ancient Egyptian proverbs and wisdom precepts on relationships and marriage:

- "Souls, Horus, son, are of the self-same nature, since they came from the same place where the Creator modeled them; nor male nor female are they. Sex is a thing of bodies not of Souls."

- "Take a wife while you are young,
  that she may make a son for you
  while you are youthful..." (Instructions of Ani)

- "When thou find sensibility of heart, joined with softness of manners, an accomplished mind, with a form agreeable to thy fancy, take her home to thy house; she is worthy to be thy friend, thy companion in life, the wife of thy bosom."

- "Remember thou art man's reasonable companion, not the slave of his passion; the end of thy being is not merely to gratify his loose desire, but to assist him in the toils of life, to soothe him with thy tenderness, and recompense his care and like treatment with soft endearments."

- "When you prosper and establish your home, love your wife with ardor. Then fill her belly and clothe her back. Caress her. Give her ointments to soothe her body. Fulfill her wishes for as long as you live. She is a fertile field for her husband. Do not be brutal. Good manners will influence her better than force. Do not contend with her in the courts. Keep her from the need to resort to outside powers. Her eye is her storm when she gazes. It is by such treatment that she will be compelled to stay in your house."

- "There is no happiness for the soul in the external worlds since these are perishable, true happiness lies in that which is eternal, within us."

- "Good things cease to be good in our wrong enjoyment of them. What nature meant to be pure sweetness, are then sources of bitterness to us; from such delights arise pain, from such joys, sorrows."

Some of what I will be discussing is contained in the book, *Sacred Sexuality: Egyptian Tantric Yoga*, and some of the images and things you will see come out of that book also. Additionally, other references will be the books *Introduction to Maat Philosophy* and *The Ancient Egyptian Wisdom Texts*.

So, with that basic caveat, I will go further now and say that some of the things that will be said are going to be undoubtedly, how should we say, designed to burst certain bubbles or certain concepts and delusions that you may have about relationships and marriage, so there's an element of poison in what will be taught here as opposed to the concepts you may have learned growing up in a decadent society of modern times. So, if you don't want your long held ideas or traditions to be poisoned, that is to say, if you don't want to give up your illusions about your concepts of relationship and your erroneous and futile ideals or your insatiable quest for fulfillment of desires as you may have come to believe those to be based on the general culture and worldly culture, and so on and so forth, if you do not want those ideas to be poisoned, to be dispelled, then you should not be listening to this program, or this series of talks. The reason is because that is one of the goals of the series, to dispel those delusions, to poison those erroneous concepts so that they will eventually die; not necessarily slowly and not necessarily fast but a progressive death.

And what is the purpose of doing that? The purpose of poisoning the illusions is so that it may be possible to fill the emptiness of illusory human desires with the fullness of spiritual enlightenment. This is the real purpose of relationships and not just for mindless pleasure or procreation, being in a family, etc. If you have any kind of illusions or delusions in life even be they wonderful ones, good ones, from a relative standpoint, positive ones, they will hold you back on your quest for spiritual enlightenment and even in your ideals of human relationships, that is to say if you have a wonderful person that you're partners with and they please you and they do everything you like and they provide for you, they never disappoint you, so called, that will be just as delusional, illusory as much as an obstacle if you have someone that you fight with all the time, that disappoints you, that annoys you.

And so, therefore, we come to the conception of the idea that this kind of talk is poison in the beginning and nectar in the end, whereas worldly pleasures and worldly sentimental relationships are nectar in the beginning and poison in the end because even those who say that they're happy in their relationships, and they may be so from a relative standpoint, they go out together and they may even finish each other's sentences and they take care of each other and so on and so forth; however, and there is always a however, in the end there is the pain of illness, of old age, letting go, death, and so on and so forth. This is what we might refer to as a worldly or egoistic, sentimental, deluded form of relationships. Those who live their lives thinking that that is the goal of life, they attain that limited goal. Those who live by a philosophical conception can have that goal in a correct way but also attain the higher goal of life which is attaining spiritual enlightenment.

So, throughout this document there are some proverbs that we will look at, which cover the themes that I just discussed that will help us along the journey of Kemetic wisdom about relationships. One important Kemetic proverb is:

> "Good things cease to be good in the wrong enjoyment of them. What nature meant to be pure sweetness are then sources of bitterness to us. From such delights our eyes pain, from such joys our eyes sorrows."

And that, in brief, is the predicament of worldly relationships. Not that you should not have pleasure, not that you should not have friendships, not that you should not get to enjoy holding hands and all that kind of thing, because seeking companionship and sex and all these kinds of things are parts of life, however, they are not all of life; the issue is the wrong enjoyment of them, the wrong understanding of them, the conception that they are the goal of life as if they were something real and abiding, where actually the opposite is true. And if you were to have an understanding, you could have enjoyments and be free from the negative aspects of them and that happens if you determine yourself to follow the Maatian Path, and that is the philosophical foundation of this talk.

HOW DID MARRIAGE COME TO BE THOUGHT OF AS IT IS TODAY?

The idea of marriage as a sacred sacrament, which comes to us today in modern culture arises from the orthodox Catholic church. It comes in with the rise of Western culture especially, where the church took upon itself the task of organizing marriage so that there would not be disorder in the society. In the beginning of Christianity the church did not control or sanction marriage and some of the early church leaders actually shunned marriage in favor of the single and celibate life. However, most people could not maintain the vows of celibacy. They found there were too many bastards running around and men were not taking care of their families, things like that, so the church leaders decided to say, "Okay. Well, marriage is a sacrament and it is governed by God and you're going to have to come to church and be married or we excommunicate you and you go to hell, etc." So, the idea of marriage as being a holy sacrament of the church was invented out of necessity. That may come as a shock to some of you but that is actually the historical record. Over centuries people have been indoctrinated into the society and its ideas of marriage and that became the tradition people believe in today for the most part. Before that, there was no governance of marriage, as such in western culture or thought of marriage as an institution, shall we call it. So marriage by the church was not in the beginning of the Christian church; it began further along in history. In the beginning, the Christian church, which became dominant and forced people within the control of the Roman empire to convert to Christianity (including Ancient Egypt by this time) shunned marriage because they thought, in some respects rightly, that it was a way of intensifying worldliness. The early church leaders were trying to follow a more austere and devotional path [even as this form of following was deficient since they only practiced reverence of the myth of Jesus and rituals around that but not the mystical philosophy side of religion]. Nevertheless, most people (including the church leaders) could not follow that path. The leaders actually tried to get people to not marry and to stay away from having sex and even castrate themselves, but they found that it didn't work because people could not control themselves then just as they cannot today. They could not control themselves in ancient times and so therefore they decided that they needed to do something about the issue. Otherwise, they were going to have a mess in terms of wayward populations, promiscuous communities and a proliferation of out of wedlock births. Therefore, they decided to institute marriage as a church sacrament.

MARRIAGE IN ANCIENT EGYPT

Now, as we go on, I wanted to introduce a couple of other concepts. Firstly, I want to delineate between the understanding of Neterian (Ancient Egyptian Religion) culture as opposed to Kemetic culture. Neterian culture is the religious side of Ancient Egyptian life, the non-secular. It includes the Shetaut Neter (Ancient Egyptian Mysteries religion), the Sebait, which is the mystical philosophy; it includes the gods and goddesses.

The Kemetic culture has a tendency more towards the secular side and this side is governed by Maat philosophy, by Maat law. And the first important lesson for you to understand about Kemetic marriage and, by extension, Kemetic relationships, is that it is covered by Kemetic culture as opposed to Neterian culture. So, in other words, you would not be expecting someone in Ancient Egypt to be going to a temple to be married by a priest. That did not happen. However, Maat secular culture and law formed a foundation for spiritual evolution as well as the secular married life.

So, how did marriage work in Ancient Egypt then? As I said before, marriage in Ancient Egypt was governed by the civil authorities and by the Maatian philosophy, the Maatian court, and essentially two people, a man and a woman, could be married by simply agreeing to do so. And it was very common to have a marriage contract that specified the legal, shall we say, the rights and sometimes responsibilities of each partner in the marital relationship. And this is very important to understand that in Ancient Egypt, the culture had developed to such a high degree that it was understood that the genders are equal and complementary in human existence; that is to say that male dominance or female dominance would be incompatible with Maatian culture, and this is part of the reason for the success of Ancient Egypt and that it allowed people to develop maturity and not to have undue stress and strain put on them by telling them that they have to get married and God is watching, if they don't stay married forever even though their family life and their personal life may be a mess and people are cheating on them and whatever, that they have to stay married because otherwise they're going to go to hell; thus all that guilt and other nonsense was invented by the church.

As a human being, a male or a female, you are the supreme arbiter and responsible entity for your existence and therefore having that capacity you also are the architect of your destiny; you create your life, and what you create becomes your fate. If you create with a burden of ignorance and falsehood and stress, then what you create will be something less than ideal and the highest ideal of attaining enlightenment will be elusive in a given lifetime, then you have to come back and do it over again as we know, and so on and so forth.

So, the ideal of marriage then is for two people who are secure in their personhood, who do not have to be subservient to the other person, people who can be mature, who can be powerful and not just mature and powerful but also comfortable in their life to choose without undue stress and without having the choice forced on you by parents or forced on you by economics or all the different kinds of pressures, artificial pressures that a society or that one's own ignorance can place on one. This can be the internal pressure from the desire to find companionship like other peers but not out of maturity but instead out of codependency, the need, sometimes desperate, to be in a paired relationship due to feeling lack or incomplete or because society says if you are not married with children you are a loser, or a less than worthy human being, etc. There can be many psychological complexes used as reasons and they lead to misery and unfulfilled relations generally. Of course, when a decision is made out of stress, delusion or ignorance, the outcome will likely be negative in the short run (present lifetime) even when it serves the higher goal of purifying the personality in the long run, through suffering.

Therefore, if one chooses to be married and one chooses to cohabitate with someone or chooses to have children and so on, then one's life has a greater chance of being fulfilled. That is, if done by mature reflection, to fulfil ordinary and sane worldly desires and inclinations, in other words, with non-coerced, non-codependent (abnormal and unhealthy psychological dependencies) reasons and without undue pressures, since, in the mature choices, one can have freedom, and one will not be doing things out of fear, fear of loss, "I'm going to lose this person and I want them," or because "I don't know if I can go away, where am I going to go, where am I going to live, how am I going to live, alone" and all those kinds of fears and insecurities. In Ancient Egypt everyone's rights and property were protected by contract and there is a maat law that all are provided with food, shelter and sustenance. So no one needed to feel compelled to live with others for economic convenience or fear or being destitute.

What they call prenuptial agreements today were very common in Ancient Egypt. It avoids the issue of finances or it would tend to prevent as much as possible, not fully but as much as possible the uncertainty of finances, the uncertainty of legal issues in a marriage and other eventualities. So people could feel more comfortable to engage in a relationship or to leave a relationship, out of choice. When you have more freedom of choice you are more comfortable taking on the amount of responsibility for a higher good out of freedom and true caring instead of out of fear and weakness. Also, you tend to your responsibility knowing the partner also has a responsibility to do theirs or that person can leave you if they're perceiving that you're not fulfilling your responsibilities and without the undue stress of the society and the church being on top of them and saying, "no, you have to stay in the marriage even if it was a mistake or the two are causing each other constant misery, etc. Of course, back then also you had a situation where it was more of a village environment and no inflated currencies raising prices constantly keeping people's nose to grindstones and constant stress. Therefore, also, there was not so much concern for children or what's going to happen to the children and broken families, etc. Life was more natural and it was all easier in a sane culture with ethical values and a truly advanced society. Additionally, you also had extended families, you had other people who understood and who did not make more of it than was necessary. So, the legal aspects of the marriage were controlled by the Maatian ideal, founded in sanity, maturity and positive social support.

Another proverb that is to be understood is related to the teaching of Aset to Heru, which states that the souls have no gender. [highlighted section by Dr. Ashby for emphasis]

> "Sex is a thing of bodies, not of souls." pain, from such joys our eyes sorrow."

And I think this is the foundation of the equality of gender in Ancient Egypt. This is one of the pillars. It is extremely important for you to understand that the manifestation of the soul in gender form, in female or male form, is merely a tendency of cosmic forces, of aryu (sum total of a person's past actions, thoughts, feelings, desires and their results) within yourself. In other words, you're manifesting as a male or a female because of the tendency of the cosmic forces that you have engendered over time in this and past lifetimes and attached yourself to. So, in one incarnation you may manifest as a woman or as a man because of certain feelings and desires that you have engendered in a previous life. In Ancient Egyptian this teaching is called "uhem ankh" – to live again, do over life once more. It is also taught in the Pert M Heru or Book of the Dead [real name Book of Enlightenment][1] And of course, if you're manifesting both in a more mixed way, you may come out physically as a hermaphrodite or you might come out as someone who's called gay or homosexual and if the aryu is of such nature you may be physically one way and mentally another, etc. The important thing to understand is all souls are beyond gender so gender is experienced the more intensely a person is attached to the physical realities of human existence and their complicated variations. That issue, of course, gets into many esoteric aspects of the Egyptian Mysteries and beyond the scope of this work at present.[2] You may go to the other books for details and extensive wisdom on those teachings. For now suffice to say that underneath it all, you're still a

---

[1] For more on the issue, see the *EGYPTIAN BOOK OF THE DEAD* by Dr. Muata Ashby
[2] For more on the issue of gender and homosexuality see the book *Conversations with God* by Dr. Muata Ashby

soul who has manifested as male and female in the past, and that is a higher reality than your physical existence and its attendant gender tendencies at present. Therefore your manifestation either as a male or female now is in no way any kind of determiner of your higher nature or a blight or a detriment to you as a human being and so therefore your value and higher nature as a soul being cannot be determined and or limited by gender.

So, with that brief historical introductory background, looking below you can see the Ancient Egyptian Hieroglyphs that are related to the Kemetic (Ancient Egyptian) concept of marriage. Let's go over those and then we'll continue to go over the other proverbs.

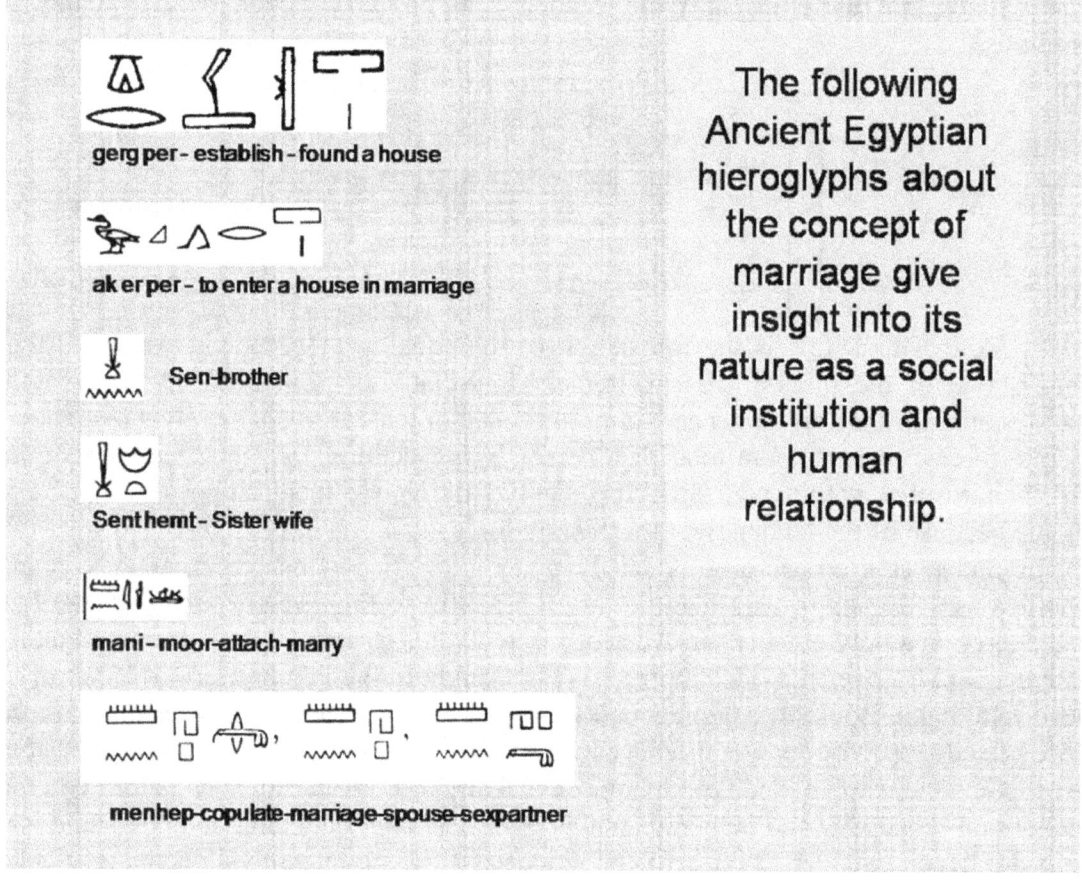

The first hieroglyphic term we will look at is "gerg per", to establish or to found a house. When two people come together to create what we call today as a marriage, it's called "gerg per" which is like starting an organization, a foundation that does work in the community; you're like a founder or somebody founds an institution or they're a founder of some organization In this case you're the founders or co-founders of a house or a home and per means –building; it's something similar to the Per in *Per Heru*. The term *ak er per* means, to go into or to enter a building with the intent of going into a marriage or a house in the form of a marriage, meaning that you're accepting and you're willingly going into a relationship, a marital relationship. Those who are men and women who are married, then also can be referred to as brothers and sisters. That should not be confused with the concept, in other countries, of incest. All human beings are kin to each other so all are brothers and sisters. Also, in Ancient Egypt there was no polygamy or polyandry (a man has several wives or the wife has several husbands).

In Ancient Egypt it was customary to marry and one could also divorce. One could divorce for a myriad of reasons including you just don't want to be married anymore or the person committed adultery or some other breach of contract, etc.; so you have that freedom. It is to be understood that in certain cases like the pharaoh, polygamy might've been allowed especially due to political reasons, because political alliances were made through marriage as much as by treaty in ancient times. But that was not a common practice of either the royalty or the general common folk of Ancient Egypt. The term for brother is *sen* and the term for a sister is *sent*. Another term that is used is *mani* depending on how it's pronounced which means to moor and it is a symbol of a boat that is wandering around, playing the field and doing whatever, but then a person who has decided to moor. So, it also means a commitment not to be promiscuous, not to be running around, and it is a choice that you're making to moor yourself as like a boat tying itself, mooring itself to a pier and not sailing the seas anymore. And then there's another term called *menhep* which means to have sexual relationships but this is in the context of a marriage. Here is a Ancient Kemetic proverb relating to sexuality:

> "Be circumspect in matters of sexual relations."

Going forward to the next proverbs now, these are actually either proverbs or they are teachings from the sages and this particular one comes from sage Ani where it says,

> "Take a wife while you're young, that she may make a son for you while you are youthful."

In Ancient Kemet, you have to realize that there is a teaching for the Initiates, the *Asaru*, and there's a teaching for the common folk, who are referred to as *rekhyt*. The rekhyt are encouraged to marry, have children and carry on a householder lifestyle if that's what they want. At some point, also, from the ranks of the rekhyt, there are going to be individuals developing spiritually, who may work for temple initiation and move beyond simple householder life. But there is no contradiction in the society, with the teaching and the worldly ideals of people. Priests and priestesses can marry and have families though, obviously, their outlook on life is dramatically different as it is guided by the Maatian teaching more closely and in a more non-secular form as opposed to that which is followed by the rekhyt. So, those who want to do more worldly things may do so within the limits of Maat secular philosophy and those who want to follow the path of the temple more closely may also do so by following the non-secular aspects of Maat Philosophy. In this context, we've shown that there were people in Ancient Egypt who ate meat and yet the teaching to the Initiates was to be vegetarian. So it is recognized that some people are at a particular level of human development while others are at another.

An me s y s a a u

No person is born being already wise.

In the same way, since every new generation of human beings needs to explore and discover their path in life, they also need to be taught the wisdom that society has amassed and assisted to adopt it for the betterment of society as a whole. So, in order for the society to continue to forge ahead, it's necessary to have new human beings coming in because human beings are always dying as well, though this idea also recognizes that not everyone is sufficiently mature enough to adopt all the wisdom and best practices as discovered by the wise leaders of society and attain enlightenment in the present lifetime. So, that's one purpose for procreation, the continuation of society. And what is the purpose of continuing society? The purpose of continuing human society is for allowing individual human beings (ignorant souls) to have an entry point into time and space so as to be able to have human experiences; for them to be able to come in and to have a venue in order to gain knowledge of self through those human experiences. From a grander perspective, it is a capacity for physical life to exist so that spirit may have a vehicle for manifesting and experiencing itself in the form of creation and interacting with itself in the forms present throughout Creation.

Moving along with the next proverb,

> "When thou find sensibility of heart, joined with softness of manners, an accomplished mind with the form agreeable to thy fancy, take her home to thy house; she is worthy to be thy friend, thy companion in life, the wife of thy bosom."

In this teaching, the sage is especially highlighting the sensibility of heart, joined with softness of manners, accomplished mind, accomplished intellect and agreeable form. So, it is giving some possible criteria for selecting a mate, not necessarily someone who is boisterous or worldly or running around all the time; and not someone who is dumb or who is like most people in this culture who revel in ignorance and faith-based culture, a culture of personality and sentimental nonsense values. An agreeable form implies someone who is appealing aesthetically, who cares about their body, which in turn means caring about health as well. However, one is not to seek a mate only on the basis of physical looks or physical appeal.

> "Remember thou art made man's reasonable companion, not the slave of his passion; the end of thy being is not merely to gratify his loose desire, but to assist him in the toils of life, to soothe him with thy tenderness and recompense his care and like treatment with soft endearments."

Now this one particularly seems to be directed to women although the other one may seem to be directed to men; it's still also directed to women as well, seeking a sensible and mature person in a man for marriage. But here, this particular proverb is reflective of the greatness of the Ancient Egyptian wisdom of marriage in that pretty much virtually, not exactly all, but virtually in every culture that we can think of, the reverse is either overtly or subtly encouraged, meaning that women are encouraged to be slaves of the passion of men and the ideal woman is the woman who doesn't nag and a woman who is ready to have sex all the time whenever the man wants to have sex, etc.; that's the male ideal that is projected in the male-oriented culture and so the woman should be a reasonable companion, a partner, and not a slave to the passions of man, and not just related to sexual passions but also whatever other passions the man may have. So in this society it's not whatever the man wants they do, and whatever he says goes, etc. This proverb is also directed to men from the standpoint that they should not be seeking a woman who would allow themselves to be manipulated or diminished. Additionally, it means that the man better behave because otherwise the woman may leave him, so this again demonstrates the independence and personal sovereignty of women in Ancient Egyptian society as well as a certain level of independence and lack of over-dependency.

So the Ancient Egyptian marriage, is supposed to be a partnership for people to help each other, on the path of life and the spiritual path to attain enlightenment, which in a higher sense are one and the same path. That's the highest goal of life, and some of the objectives towards that goal may include working so you can have a nice house that you can live in; nice from the standpoint of not expensive and big but nice that you're going to be comfortable, so that you have all your practical physical needs met and everyone works to do their part, not that one works and brings in income while the other sits around and neither should be a slave –to the other or to the work ethic of the Western culture that the male is supposed to work and produce the bread and the woman is supposed to stay at home or that both should work and have no life. Some cultures may go even further and still believe in the adage that, a "woman should stay barefoot and pregnant" all the time, etc.

That is all nonsense from the perspective of Kemetic Marriage; that is all ignorance, all concepts of an ignorant Western, barbarous or worldly or primitive culture that has not matured to the level of Ancient Egyptian culture. This is how advanced Ancient Egyptian culture was and through us it can resurge to a level that we can manifest even now. So, it's important for men to understand these principles and it's important for women to understand as well so that they can have a balanced and well-adjusted relationship, and so that they will not be relying on each other for happiness or for pleasures that are inordinate and thereby avoid the pitfalls of ignorant and immature relationships.

Naturally, people want to please each other; they want to make each other happy and things like that and that is a normal aspect of egoistic human existence, the desire to make another happy so that one can feel good about oneself by giving joy to another and receiving pleasure from a happy person, etc. On the receiving end, the joy felt by having someone care for one is also needed for certain aspects of the personality's evolution and development of self-worth, etc. But the inordinate pursuit of that pleasure-seeking and pleasure-giving so as to feel happy or fulfilled through egoistic human relations leads to emotional imbalance, intensification of ego either when things go well or when emotional support or pleasure is withdrawn for any reason (intentional or otherwise) and to ultimate disaster in terms of relationship deterioration. If people work together, they can produce great things; if one group of people try to impose themselves on others, try to enslave others, it leads to a emotional, ethical, and spiritual disaster for themselves and for the enslaved.

The next teaching is,

> "When you prosper and establish your home, love your wife with ardor. Then fill her belly and clothe her back. Caress her. Give her ointments to soothe her body. Fulfill her wishes for as long as you live. She is a fertile field for her husband. Do not be brutal. Good manners will influence her better than force. Do not contend with her in the courts. Keep her from the need to resort to outside powers. Her eye is her storm when she gazes. It is by such treatment that she will be compelled to stay in your house."

Of course, these apply to the males and females, for the males and females to treat each other with warmth and with kindness and to doing what you can to meet the necessities, not necessarily the desires, of the other person. Necessities are a normal and "necessary" part of life while desires can be for inordinate and ultimately detrimental things. A child needs nutritious food but may desire candy. Providing the necessary nutrients is proper and will tend to perpetuate the relationship with health over a long time while providing the sweets for short-term pleasure and satisfaction will, in a short time, lead to disease and ultimately damage the relationship. And again, a caution is provided for men who are generally physically stronger than females; that difference in physical capacities is not meaningful as to the worth of either, as a human being, but rather a difference for complementary social interactions and progress. So it is a permission to physically dominate, hit women or be verbally abusive or otherwise hurtful. Instead, men should strive to use reason and or calm, during interactions, while trying to reach a resolution based on truth and justice (maat) instead of egoistic personal desires or delusions of superiority. If these injunctions were to be followed honestly and forthrightly then there should be little reason to resort to going to court over disputes. Rather, the ethical conscience demands following the spirit of the Maatian wisdom as reflected in a Kemetic Marriage Contract and that should allow you to work things out in an amicable manner with reason and truth and Maatian (justice) order that will lead to HTP or peace before, during and after the relationship is over.

Kemetic Guide to Creating Positive Relationships and a Kemetic Marital Agreement

The aforesaid applies to those who are in a mature and balanced relationship, not for those of you who may be listening to this in the future or even now who are in relationships where you're imbalanced, where you are involved with a person who is worldly or who is unrighteous or mentally unstable. etc. You may have to go to court and let the court deal with things. But this is for those of you who may be entering into a relationship with a person who is initiated into this ideal philosophy and who agree with this ideal, this culture of maat wisdom. You should work to have amicable relations as you're entering into as well as exiting a relationship. For those who are in relationships already and only now becoming initiated into this Kemetic Marriage philosophy, you need to learn it well and work together, dealing with both of your egoisms, to a point where you can both agree to its benefits in principle, in spirit and legally also; so for anyone who wants to adopt this teaching, if you do and if you go all the way to creating a premarital Kemetic Marriage Contract, you should also agree that if a time comes when there is a need to break up that you will follow the parameters in the contract as your legal path instead of going to settle things with lawyers in the courts. In other words, the Kemetic Marriage Contract will be your legal agreement and it can be filed with the courts as well just as any regular prenup agreement would in the ordinary society.

In this context then, you should try to see the other person, as I said here, as a fertile field and yourself for that person as well. The relationship with the other person is a venue for theirs and your inner self to develop in. This is the real purpose of having a relationship. And the reason why you enter into a relationship is to fulfill a gap, to fulfill something that is missing, which is not filled by the other person but is filled by your discovering it within yourself by means of the experiences and wisdom attained through relationships. For example, discovering inner peace and self-worth may occur in a conducive relationship where one is confronted with experiences that necessitate exploring and cultivating those aspects of the personality, etc.

Now, of course, all this can get distorted in many different ways. Women can come to feel that men are dogs and they can come to feel that women are cats and men can feel that women are there mainly for their pleasure and women can feel that the men are there for their use, to take care of them and to provide for them so that they can live their lives, have children, etc., and to that extent, they service the needs of men. This is a selfish utilitarian view of relationships. It's a very degraded kind of conception of life and it's very ego intensifying as well which leads to people in such relationships moving farther away from enlightenment and more towards the creation of negative worldly *Aryu* that is full of sorrow and pain and discord.

Another Ancient Egyptian proverb that I would add to the list is,

> "There is no happiness for the soul in the external worlds since these are perishable, indiscernible true happiness lies in that which is eternal, within us."

And, of course, that which is eternal within us is the soul. Since the gender of an individual is illusory and the soul is the true higher nature of self, you cannot expect to find abiding happiness in any relationship but with that same higher self. No matter how wonderful it may seem to work out; no matter how great, like I said before, you may seem to go hand in hand and you're soulmates and you finish each other's sentences and all that kind of thing, it's all illusory because it's perishable and changeable. Anything that is changeable and perishable is illusory. Anything that is illusory will inevitably lead to loss and pain if it is leaned upon as one's source of happiness and not treated with maat, realizing its true nature and purpose. If it's treated, as I said before, with the correct understanding, then there will be a right enjoyment of it, there will be a positive experience through it and that is the ideal of the Kemetic Marriage and that will be a Maatian foundation for you to develop into a kind of personality that is capable and suitable for higher initiation and higher spiritual development. That is an introduction to the philosophy behind the Kemetic marriage. Now in this document there is a sample of a Kemetic marriage contract or agreement.

Figure 1: An Ancient Egyptian Family

There is an important teaching relevant to Ancient Egyptian iconography related to the Kemetic family. In the image above you can see a husband and a wife and a little boy and a little girl. You'll notice that the males are painted in red and the females are painted in white and that is not at all to be taken to mean that the Ancient Egyptians were red and white. That is ridiculous. That is nonsense. The idea is that this is an idealistic portrayal. In iconographical portrayals you have idealistic and you have naturalistic portrayals. The naturalistic shows people in their original, true hues, their skin color and we find them in either dark black or brown or light brown as Ancient Egyptians. As for the red and white color, red symbolizes spirit in this context and white symbolizes creation. The union of the two, like the symbol of the ankh, a circle tied with a vertical line, relates to the coming together of spirit with matter to create life.

Figure 2: An Ancient Egyptian Ankh symbol

    In this way, the male and female genders complement each other; the spirit that goes into matter and creates a living existence through a child. A child is seen in this context as an androgynous idea of life as opposed to a male or a female. As the child develops from an embryo, it differentiates into a gender.

    HETEP

Chapter 1: The Process of Constructing a Kemetic Marital Agreement (Kemetic Marriage Contract)

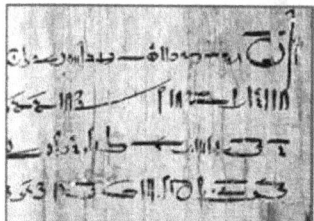

Figure 3: Part of an Ancient Egyptian Marriage Contract written in the Demotic Script (oriental Institute) Marriage contract, Late Period, Dynasty 365, 380–364 b.c.
[In thi case, the document specifies that the man must provide the wife a set amount silver and grain each year and that he must do so regardless of where she is living in the case of divorce.]

marriage contract between the priest Pagosh and Teteimhotep Ptolemaic Period, 172 BC

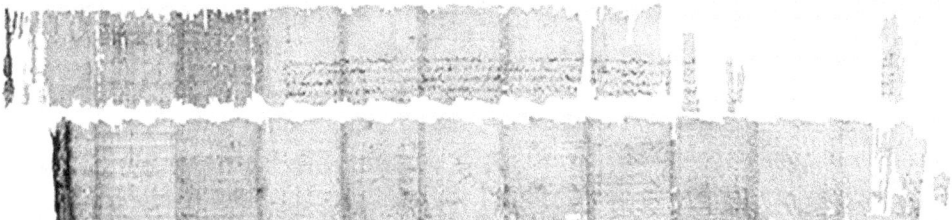

Marriage contract, Late Period, Dynasty 30, 380–343 b.c.

Firstly, it is recommended that you view and study the lecture series Kemetic Marriage and Relationships 2011 by Sebai Dr. Muata Ashby (www.Egyptianyogabooks.com). That series will provide you the in depth and fundamental philosophical teaching upon which Kemetic Marriage was and is based. This guide has been prepared, in part, based on that series, to help you apply the knowledge gained from that lecture series. This guide has been prepared for helping you go through a process of *three phases* in order to create a marital agreement (contract) with your prospective partner.

Keep in mind that in this program you are working to create a marital agreement so that your rights and reasonable needs may be met by the relationship in keeping with the principles of Kemetic relationships and marriage. In this way you are seeking not only to satisfy your needs, but you also need to keep in mind how you will protect the rights and needs of your partner. In this way you will have the highest chance to be fulfilled by the relationship, and at the same time honor and help your partner to achieve his/her goals.

In ancient times, living together out of wedlock and having sex out of wedlock and using contraceptives out of wedlock or within wedlock were accepted evolved practices of a mature society. However, adultery, promiscuity and having children out of marriage were severely discouraged and were considered to be against the precepts of Maat (the law).

The first thing to consider before entering into a marital agreement with anyone is: Is this person honorable? Or is the person immature, dishonest, irresponsible, etc.? If the person is not honorable you should reconsider your decision to enter into marriage with the person as such negative qualities do not bode well for the success of marriage.

The success of a marriage is not to be gauged by how many children are produced or how much wealth is built up or how much sex there is. Rather, it should be assessed on its capacity to lead the married people to inner peace, and fulfillment of life's purpose: Spiritual Enlightenment. If the marriage will be producing struggles and strife, why add more of that to your life?

Another question to consider is: Is the person a bum, or do they have responsible goals, a trade or profession to develop their skills and working life and to provide their share of income? If the person is floundering around without direction, you should not think that you will change them or that they will figure it out later. These are delusions; you are fooling yourself because you want to overlook the person's flaws because you are attracted to them and want to be with them. If you proceed, then you have no one but yourself to blame for problems that may arise due to this issue. Also, remember that if you are not honest in this process of expressing your concerns and hopes for the relationship, you will dishonor yourself and your partner by allowing weaknesses in the relationship to exist whereby negative situations and actions may occur that will lead to annoyance, sufferings, etc., in the relationship. Not all items can be included since not everything can be thought of and the future will bring new knowledge about yourself and your partner. The effort is to establish a solid foundation based on your current knowledge of yourself and your knowledge of the teachings in order to provide the highest chance for success.

Non-negotiable Maatian principles:

The Kemetic marital agreement was, in ancient times, and is today based on Ancient Egyptian Maat Philosophy. The marital agreement will relate to certain maatian and personal principles that both partners value and will want to acknowledge, protect and observe. There are certain non-negotiable principles (Maat ethics) that all followers of Kemetic culture must agree to follow. The Precepts of Maat are non-negotiable principles that all must agree to observe and make a good-faith effort to follow. The 42 precepts may be classified into six major principles and within these more can be subdivided. The six principles are Truthfulness, Non-violence, Right Action, Right Thinking, Non-stealing and Sex Sublimation. The subdivisions are under Right Action. They are Selfless Service to Humanity, Right Speech and Right Worship of the Divine or Correct Spiritual Practice.

42 Precepts of Maat related teachings [number in parenthesis is the specific precept of Maat]	Principles of Ethical Social Conscience
Truth (1), (6), (7), (9), (24)	Honesty
Non-violence (2), (3), (5), (12), (25), (26), (28), (30), (34)	Gentleness, congeniality, friendliness, peacefulness

Non-stealing (4), (8), (10)	Respect for property, persons
Self-Control-Right Action (Living in accordance with the teachings of Maat) (15), (20), (22), (36)	Balanced character, prone to do what is right
Selfless Service, (29)	Helping partner and others to lead a better life
Right Speech (11), (17), (23), (33), (35), (37)	Speaking with honesty, accuracy, goodness
Right Worship (13), (21), (32), (38), (42)	Uphold spiritual values
Balance of Mind - Reason - Right Thinking (14), (16), (18), (31), (39), (41)	Clear thinker, capacity for logical thinking, capacity for higher learning
Sex-Sublimation (19), (27)	Well adjusted, normal sex interest, interest in satisfying needs of partner but also in discovering elevated aspects of sex energy

The Non-negotiable Maatian principles are mandatory and all parties must agree to uphold these. Your discussion will help you to fully understand them and allows your prospective partner to know you understand them and are pledging to uphold them.

The Two Paths in Life

- Ancient Egyptian proverb:
- "There are two roads traveled by humankind, those who seek to live MAAT and those who seek to satisfy their animal passions."

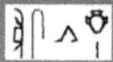 *Shems-ab* – "followers desire of one's heart-desire, greed, lust, wishes."

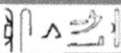 *Shems-maat* – "followers desire of truth, order, justice, righteousness."

From the 42 Precepts of MAAT:
  (1) "I have not done iniquity." Variant: Acting with falsehood.

 *Sheps* – "nobility, honor, venerable-ness, honored ancestors."

"Maligning others is abhorred by the KA."
-Ancient Egyptian proverb:

Non-negotiable personal principles:

As one matures, one discovers ways of life and personal standards that one has learned to live by. For example, you may have grown up watching your friends be promiscuous and getting STD's. You may have reflected and decided that is not a lifestyle you want to accept. This is then a personal standard that you will not negotiate. Will you live with a person who plays music late at night when you want to meditate or do spiritual studies? Will you want to be with a person who will be nagging you about having children when you do not want children or vice versa? Do you want to be married to a person whose personal standards you do not like?

Ideally, one should not allow one's feelings to be deeply engaged with another person until one is sure that one wants to enter into a full marital agreement. However, many times these issues are not reflected upon prior to becoming emotionally attached or and entering marriage, and the two partners are unable to handle their emotions or and to act on each other's principles; hence the high divorce rate in the western culture (especially the USA). Clearly, it is best for these issues to be reflected upon and negotiated before deep emotional connections are made, unless the two prospective partners are able to handle their emotions and act on principle, even after they have become attached emotionally and then have found out about a major flaw in their prospective partner.

So, if there are any non-negotiable items that cannot be agreed upon, or if there are any personal principles you cannot live with, you should reconsider whether the marital relationship with that person is wise for you at this time. Working through this guide will assist in that reflection.

Honoring Self and Exercising Freedom while Honoring the Feelings of the Other Person and Handling Conflict

In the marital experience, there may be times when you feel that the other person is not acceding to your desires or demands. Sometimes you may find that there are pathways you feel you need to take that relate to your personal or professional development that the other person may not agree with. You may feel the need to proceed with those actions regardless of the objections of the other person, and that may cause strain in a relationship. Firstly, before you take such action, you should be sure that it does not violate the precepts of Maat. Next you should take care that it does not violate the spirit of the Marital Agreement. Sometimes one person in a relationship may be growing faster than another who may remain cautious or apprehensive. This is a time when respect and honor and individual fortitude are necessary to allow other people the chance to follow their path (within the context of a marriage and within parameters that do not violate non-negotiable principles). People need to have the freedom to grow in as well as outside of a relationship. This is important because as you allow others the latitude to pursue their goals, they will allow and assist you in pursuing yours. For example: One person may want to go to Africa to pursue research while the other person does not want them to go because they will feel lonely. The trip is a legitimate personal development issue and does not violate the family finances, leave children unattended for an inordinate period of time, etc. The person needing the research should pursue that and the person staying behind needs to face their inordinate attachment feelings and also work on pursuing their own legitimate agenda for personal or professional development. So your agreement should keep these concepts as an overall framework for the spirit of the agreement. The marital contract is not to be created with the idea of shackling or controlling another person, and not to tie down people who do not want to be together otherwise. It is a purposeful and willing (by your choice/volition) agreement whereby two mature and responsible people agree to certain restrictions and regulations for the purpose of honoring, helping and being able to love each other in freedom and without the burden of worry about the uncertainty of conflicts, affairs, betrayals, loneliness, etc. Remember, you are choosing to moor (Kemetic definition of Marriage) yourself to this port for all the benefits that can be derived, including companionship, sex, collaboration to build wealth, to produce progeny, help in old age, and assisting each other to attain grow spiritually, and to attain spiritual enlightenment, the goal of life, etc. However, the other person's feelings and thoughts should be taken into consideration carefully whenever a unilateral action is to be taken. And you should be prepared to extend the same right that you feel is appropriate to handle your personal issues, to the other person. And you should also be prepared for the possibility that the other person may not accept your choices and may decide to exercise their right for divorce, which either of you can exercise at any time and for any reason.

Handling conflicts constructively

→ An important aspect of the proposal is a provision for handling conflicts. If you plan on this, you will reduce the incidences of inevitable conflicts damaging the marital relations (i.e., maintain friendship between partners).

→ You may include provisions such as: *we will have weekly or monthly discussions about the state of our plans and go over each other's concerns*. This is a way of preempting problems, but what if problems arise unexpectedly?

→ In such cases you may try to work them out when they arise, but that may not be possible sometimes for varied reasons: the kids may need to be taken care of, one or both partners may need to go to work, etc.

→ So the preferred manner to handle issues in such cases is to schedule a time (if it is an urgent matter then schedule ASAP) to have the discussion about the issue so that it does not disturb the peaceful relations the rest of the time.

→ If it is a contentious matter that needs to be discussed, then apply more structure and formality to the discussion such as is suggested in the PREP method (use the speaker-listener technique explained and demonstrated in the book and DVDs, *Fighting For Your Marriage* (www.prepinc.com).

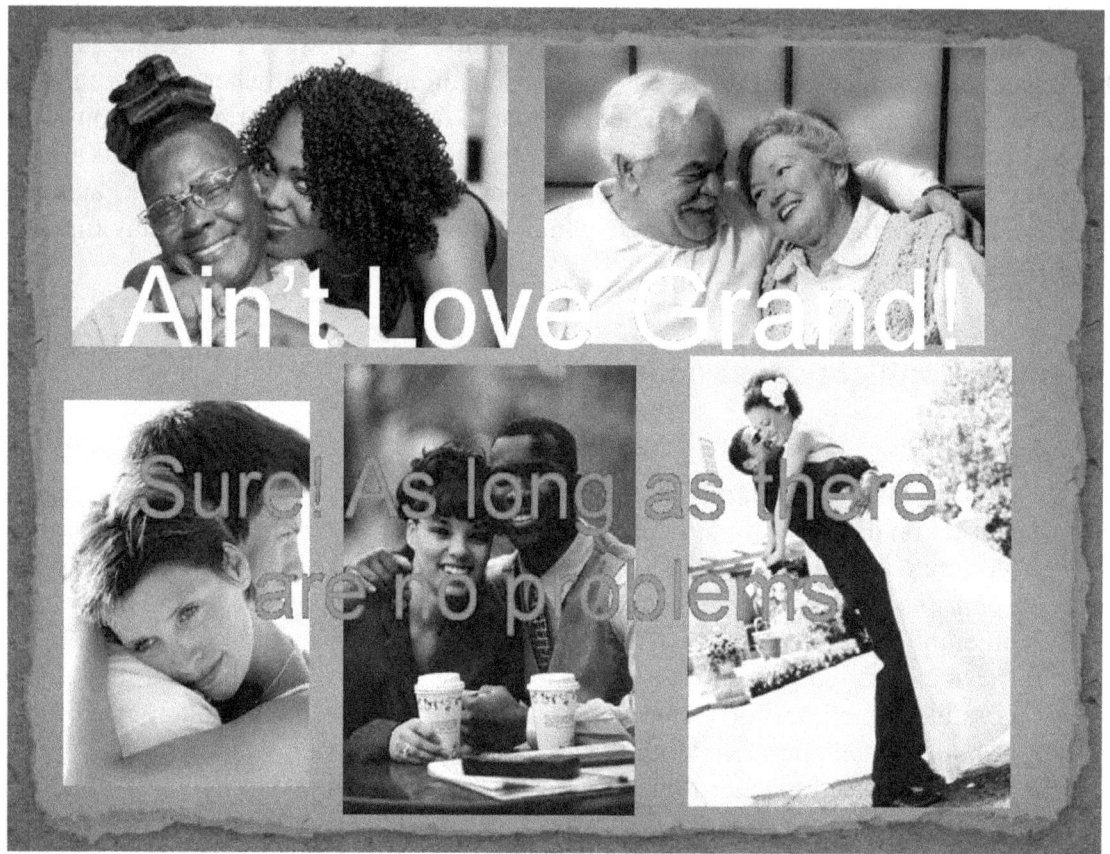

Notes of Caution and Honoring the Spirit of the Marital Agreement:

If it were possible to have no problems in a relationship, there would be no need for agreements; but because human beings are flawed and because the world of time and space itself is illusory[3], there will always be some problems in life. The wise person prepares to handle problems that WILL occur, just as people prepare for storms that they know will come and hit their city, instead of having blind faith on illusory events of life. The creation of an agreement, no matter how altruistic sounding, does not guarantee success in marriage. It does provide a framework, a foundation and guidelines for helping a relationship succeed. This means that since human beings have aryu (sum total of desires, feelings, and thoughts accumulated over this and many lifetimes (what Hindus and others call *Karma*) and since the realm of time and space is ever changeable, perfection should not be expected from flawed human beings. However, major violations of ethical conscience cannot be passed over as unreasonable expectations.

Another important point is that a marital contract should not be used as an instrument for fault-finding. Fault-finding is actively and constantly looking to catch your partner in some violation no matter how minimal it might be. Being human (combination of soul and body) and existing in time and space, there is bound to be some error at any given point. But, the idea is that there should be no violation of major items such as the non-negotiable principles and for the errors that do arise there should be a good faith effort to recognize the error and then work on correcting it. In this way the partner and the relationship itself works to elevate a person's ari and enhance their chances of leading a maatian life and attaining Nehast.

Additionally, one of the aims of the marital contract is to equalize the rights and responsibilities of each partner and not for enforcing one partner on or over another. However, there are some areas where each person has primacy of rights. For example, in matters of pregnancy and childbirth, both husband and wife have a say, but in terms of pregnancy, the female has the final word because this activity relates to her body. However, as another example, suppose the female partner agreed to have a child in the marital contract, but later decides she does not wish to have one. If all other parameters are favorable†, the husband has the right to divorce for the purpose of finding someone else with whom to have a child.

†[For example: If the living situation is not stable (homeless, economic or other uncertainty), the female would have the right not to have a child, and the husband would need to agree with that decision, as it would be based on Maatian ethics.]

---

[3] See the book *Egyptian Yoga The Philosophy of Enlightenment* by Dr. Muata Ashby

It is also important to understand that it is not necessary or demanded that each partner should agree on everything in life. It is healthy to have different points of view so as to be able to use the virtues of each gender to discover the best paths as a cooperative team. However, in reference to the contract, it is important to have agreement on the main aspects of the relationship so that there may be a common foundation for both of your main goals and objectives. So you may not both have exactly all the same goals, but you announce your differences up front so you can both know what they are, and how the other person wants to have them respected, and you can also have yours respected as well. For example: one may be interested in working with children while the other is interested in forestry. So knowing this, both will need to agree to live where the two objectives can be pursued simultaneously or consecutively, as part of a concerted plan to meet the needs of each partner (considerations may include such things as: if a college degree is necessary, or where they need to live geographically, etc.) and with the income that those endeavors can produce. Additionally, it is alright to have different opinions about varied aspects of life, but there should be agreement on the major aspects as outlined in this guide. For example, one may like sunsets while the other may like dawns. You should not expect agreement on all details of likes and dislikes, so allowances should be made for people to have integrity in their individuality and respect for their opinions, even if they are different from one's own: this is honoring the person. It is important to understand that because all are essentially expressions of the Divine, and because the Divine is infinite, it is possible to have varied modes of vision about the same ultimate truth. Therefore, while the visions of different mystics may on the surface appear to be divergent, if they are examined more deeply, the commonality of vision may be revealed. So too, the opinions and feelings of others should be examined in this way to see if there is real divergence, or if their vision is simply a different perspective on the same truth, like when children see pictures of their parents in varied activities, at work, at home, at the beach, at the store, different children may prefer one picture over another, but they all love their parents as they are recognized to be the same regardless of the varied modes in which they are being seen. Furthermore, it is important, again, to understand that you may be an advocate for one another, but you cannot save the other person from all errors or failures. They cannot save you either. You therefore need to cultivate detachment and dispassion, being an advocate, but not a shield, trying to prevent others from certain experiences they need to grow on their own. You can be a counsel and offer what you think is wise, but sometimes people need to experience the erroneous results and consequences of their actions-if there are to be any (since it is also possible that you may be wrong in your assessment of what you feel to be their error).

Handling Minor infractions of the agreement

This is an example of a provision you may add to the agreement. For example, what if one of you comes home after a long day and makes a rude comment to the partner. This happened due to stress. A solution may be the person who made the rude comment may realize the error and apologize immediately. If they did not realize what they did, it can be pointed out and an apology can be accepted, and then allow the person time to regenerate themselves (time in silence, meditation, shower and sleep, etc.). Or, the partner can recognize the other person is stressed out and make a mental note or actually write it down (date, time, what occurred, etc.) and bring it up at the next couple's meeting, or request a specific couple's meeting to discuss this incident.

Handling Major infractions of the agreement

Using the example above: If rude comments becomes a habit, you may wish to practice formal communications (speaker-listener technique) to communicate about the issue. You may want to engage counseling. If the problem persists and the other person does not want to change the behavior after reasonable efforts, the person whose rights were violated may have justification to call for divorce. Other major infractions would be violation of any of the Non-negotiable Maatian principles or a Non-negotiable Personal Principles. Remember that if you allow serious infractions, you are complicit in the degradation of your relationship and your own personality.

DIVORCE:

Sometimes one of the partners may violate the agreement in such a way that the relationship or the agreement cannot be sustained. Or perhaps the two partners matured and realized that they grew sufficiently together and would now like to pursue other horizons. In such cases, divorce is permissible. However, if the decision for the divorce is not mutual, the person initiating the divorce has additional responsibilities to make sure that the rights and wellbeing of the person they are leaving are protected and provided for.

STEPS FOR ARRIVING AT A MARITAL AGREEMENT

Step 1: You are to create a list of issues [*main proposal statements*] that you think are important for the kind of Kemetic relationship you would like to have with your prospective partner.

Step 2: Next you will have a discussion with your partner where each point that you listed and each point that your partner listed will be discussed.

Step 3: For each point in the list you will come to: A- agreement [consensus of what you both think is reasonable], B-disagreement, C-compromise

> If a disagreement arises on a Non-negotiable Maatian principle, it must be resolved by both partners agreeing to abide by Maa, or the relationship/marriage should not proceed. The couple may seek to consult with the priest or priestess of Maat and to gain insight into the Maatian principle governing the issue.
>
> If this is disagreement on a Non-negotiable Personal Principle, it must also be resolved. If a compromise cannot be reached, the couple may consult with the priest or priestess of Maat and to gain insight into the Maatian principle governing the issue and each other's point of view on the matter. If there is continued disagreement, the relationship/marriage should not proceed.
>
> If this item is not one of the Non-negotiable Maatian or one of the Non-negotiable Personal principles, and the two parties cannot reach a mutually acceptable compromise about the issue, the couple may consult with the priest or priestess of Maat and then reopen discussions.
>
> If this item is not one of the Non-negotiable Maatian or Non-negotiable Personal principles, and you cannot reach agreement (negotiated way of handling the issue), you may cease negotiations or you may accept the non-resolution of the issue and move forward with the rest of the agreement if other items are agreed upon. However, this is not recommended, because the irresolution can open the door to erosion of the integrity of the relationship through continuing arguments and the gradual degradation of the relations. The 42 Precepts of Maat cover virtually all situations in life, so the inability to reach some mutually acceptable understanding on the matter, among persons who purport to follow the Kemetic path, may signal a serious ignorance about the path, serious flaw(s) of ethics and thus character, or serious unwillingness to commit to a marital relationship, any of which should point to reconsideration of the person as a viable marital partner.

Step 4: Now you can list the points that are acceptable to you both and that will become your premarital agreement that you will use to guide your relationship as you move forward with your marriage.

Your marriage begins when you both sign the final agreement. You may marry each other in a civil court for legal purposes or by an ordained Kemetic priest or priestess. However, you are both agreeing that this final agreement is the highest authority for determining the disposition of your marriage.

Qualities of an Ideal Neterian Relationship

- Grow in independence
- Grow in detachment
- Grow in honor
- Ethical Conscience
- Partner, not mate—Desiring to be with someone to satisfy a void will not work without foundation in self—if don't need to satisfy a void then can relate on other levels
- Reasonable expectations
- Assistance, not preceptorship
- Physical and emotional support, not substitute
- Do out of choice and self-satisfaction
- Importance of having a viable career interest in line with maatian ideals
- Not spend all time together
- Never fall in love, rather share heart but only with the righteous, those who value and uphold truth
- Compatible Goal of life
- Compatible religious perspectives

Qualities of an Ideal Neterian Relationship Cont.

- Redirect anger: this is what I did to myself, through my ignorance, the illusoriness of the world, 'stop
- Tantra-Men need to learn to be more female-sensitivity-when hear of need try to meet it– needs not wants (can never be fulfilled by time and space)
- Tantra-women need to learn to be more male-not expect men to be psychic – not expect perfection-expect them to listen to rationality with reasonable limits
- Heru and Set
- Men do not dismiss women as emotional
- Women do not dismiss men as uncaring

CHAPTER 2: GUIDING QUESTIONS TO HELP YOU WORK THROUGH THE ISSUES AND ARRIVING AT A FINAL AGREEMENT

The Guiding Questions are to be used with the "WORKSHEETS" section of this manual to help you bring up and discuss the pertinent issues and arrive at agreements.

MAJOR KEMETIC PRINCIPLES FOR RELATIONSHIPS	Guiding questions for meeting your needs. Guiding questions for how do you think you should protect the needs and wellbeing of your partner also.
Non-negotiable Maatian principles	Is there agreement with both partners to uphold non-negotiable Maatian principles? [Note, if the answer is no, there is no need to proceed further, as these principles are the basis of a Kemetic relationship. The relationship should be ended or postponed until the partner who cannot agree to the principles further studies Maat philosophy and teachings, and is counseled by a Kemetic priest/priestess on this matter, to see if this will help give a better basis of understanding for the person, and if the person is able to practice the principles consistently for an extended period of time [perhaps for 6 months or 1 year or however long both parties are willing to wait].
Honor	How would you like to be treated? How would you like to be addressed? How will you uphold and protect the honor of your partner's soul?
Religion/Spiritual Affiliation(s) (see the lecture series for more guidance on this issue)	What religion you will follow? If you will both follow Shetaut Neter then which teacher or tradition of KMT religion will be followed…one or more? Will these be authentic? If you both will follow Shetaut Neter then you may skip the following questions. Is it okay for your spouse to follow a different religion? If both parents follow different religions, what religion will the children be raised in, what rituals of each parent's religion will the child partake of, and is this okay with both parents?
Sex	How often? Types/Styles/Acceptable positions?

	What conditions? Contraception? Testing for STD's? How to promote satisfaction of both? Will sex be allowed to be used as a manipulation tool to control the partner?
Finances	How will you provide income? How will you save and invest? How should family moneys be budgeted? Is there a level of purchase beyond which the other partner should be consulted?

	More Guiding questions:
	
	1. How will savings and investment programs be evaluated?
	2. Is this a viable investment program? (in line with maatian principles)
	3. Will one or both make investment decisions? Or will one be in charge and the other will give consent?
	4. How will investment profits be handled?
	    a. Will it go into a joint account?
	    b. Or individual account?
	    c. Or a budget account to pay bills?
	    d. Will some go into a secondary (short or long term) investment account?
	5. Where will main savings be kept? (What kind of account? In what currency? In what country?)
	6. If there are any major projects that affect the whole family (ex. buy a house, a car, etc.), how will decisions be made to make those purchases?
	7. If one partner does not agree with an investment or a purchase will you proceed anyway or will one partner be able to veto an action (without resentment by the other partner)?
	8. All families should have a budget to meet the basic expenses and long term goals of the family. How will the budget be setup? Who will manage it?
	9. Will there be one joint checking/savings account for both or a joint account and also separate personal

	accounts for discretionary spending by each individually? 10. What if partners separate, will the account remain open and will they continue and divide proceeds of profits? Or will it be closed and they open separate accounts? 11. If one or both die, what will be done with the portion of the deceased partner's funds?
Children	How many will have? How will be reared? Is it expected that one parent will become a stay at home parent to rear the child(ren)? If yes, which parent will do so? How will they be schooled? What forms of discipline will be applied and supported by both parents? What religion will be taught? How to deal with family members following different religions or traditions who may impose their way on the children? What country(ies) will they grow up in? What friends will they be allowed to have? If one partner or both die, what is to happen to the children?
Resolution of conflicts	What steps to handle disagreements? How to handle hurt feelings?
	How to handle what one feels are major infractions of Non-negotiable Maatian principles by one's partner?
	How to handle what one feels are major infractions of Non-negotiable Personal principles by one's partner?
	How to handle what one feels are major infractions to the agreement?
	How to handle what one feels are minor infractions to the agreement?
	How to handle NEW non-negotiable personal principles that arise during the relationship—after this marital agreement has been established? If new issues arise will you discuss the issues and agree on them and then add them to the marriage contract as addendums?
	Regular Meetings: It is helpful and healthful to the marriage to have regular meetings to see how the agreement is working out and to bring u any issues that may need to be resolved. You may schedule annual. Monthly or weekly meetings in

	accordance with your needs.
Chores and household duties	How will these be handled?
Divorce	What would be grounds for Divorce? Will both parties seek marital counseling prior to becoming divorced? If so, how many sessions before a decision is rendered? If children are involved, will the children receive counseling by a qualified therapist/counselor before and during the divorce, and even after if needed? Will the children be treated in a manner that they are not put in the middle, and where both parents agree to speak about each other respectfully and treat each other respectfully in the children's presence and when speaking to the children privately about the other parent as well? How will the children be looked after? How will visitation rights be setup? How will finances be handled if both agree to divorce? How will finances be handled if both do not agree to divorce but one wants the divorce? Will the person bringing the divorce compensate for that?
Death	If a partner dies, how will their affairs be handled?
Health	What lifestyle will be pursued? Will the Kemetic diet be implemented? What healers/doctors will use? If one partner gets sick and cannot speak for themselves how will their desires be handled? If one partner is incapacitated how would they want the partner to handle their treatment?
Other:	

CHAPTER 3: INSTRUCTIONS FOR DEVELOPING YOUR PROPOSALS THAT WILL BE REFLECTED UPON FIRST & THEN HOW TO DISCUSS THEM WITH YOUR PROSPECTIVE PARTNER AND THEN ARRIVE AT THE FINAL AGREEMENT WITH YOUR PARTNER

Here you will create your proposal items that you will discuss/negotiate with your prospective partner.

The next part of the manual contains worksheets for you to make notes about what you want to propose to your prospective partner. It is setup in such a way to help you work through the major principles that should be covered in a Kemetic Marriage Contract. In many ways, the first principle is the most important as it sets the tone and parameters for the rest. Therefore, we will spend a little extra time discussing and describing how the first principle is to be proposed, discussed and how the elements of this principle can be agreed to by both parties. The same method will apply to the other principles. If you have any difficulties you may consult with a Maatian priest(ess) or lawyer.

At this stage you are trying to propose certain ideas to your prospective partner and you should want them to be as clearly understood as possible. For this purpose though I would suggest not using a prose format, and rather instead use an outline, term paper format, thesis proposal – or a contract format. The reason for the suggestion is that I think the purpose and intent, and also the specific proposal ideas, will come out more clearly. Also, in order to avoid negative tones or connotations, you should also preface each proposal statement with the words: "*I would like to propose…*" or similar. This will keep the statement on track and prevent the possibility of misunderstandings that could arise with statements like "We will do this…" "Things will work like this…" which could convey a demanding or disrespectful or imposing tone. Also, try to be specific with your proposal statements and try to not allow your specific feelings and desires to be embedded in the prose of your writing as general ideas or vague concepts. Remember these are not only the parameters you want the relationship to work within, but you need to allow your prospective partner to understand what you want and also need in order for the relationship to work for you – so you need to know what you want and what you specifically need to do because you will need to try to live up to that also. Also, it is easier to achieve goals and avoid strife when we know what we are about and what we want as opposed to going on hope or good wishes for things to work out in the end.

The elements of this principle will be the *main proposal statements* (1., 2., 3., etc.) and these may be followed by brief explanatory statements that may provide insight into why the main proposal statements are important to you or you feel they are important for the relationship. (a.). Example:

1. I would like to propose that we use respect and proper conduct in relation to how we treat each other.
    a. So we can agree to disagree on certain points, knowing that we both have good intentions and we are seeking to live and operate within the boundaries of Maat. We do not have to agree on everything all the time, but allowing that as we mature and develop, we will discover greater truths, we need not impose our particular truth on each other since we are both of good will and mean well for each other, and do not want to impose unreasonable constrictions on each other that we may not be ready to understand and or accept.

2. I would like to propose that we address each other in kindness and gentleness as much as possible.
    a. Specifically, I would like us to address each other with gentle words, to catch each other's attention when necessary without needing to resort to harsh words. If for any reason we forget ourselves and one of us uses an untoward word, I would like to propose that we recognize that that occurred not out of malice, but out of forgetfulness or stress and that it was not meant maliciously. If one needs time to reflect, that will be allowed and we will agree to meet on any outstanding issue that arose in order to resolve it as soon as possible.

3. Etc...
    a. Etc...

You are not necessarily expected to go through this entire process of creating a Kemetic marriage contract on your own. You may avail yourself of the books and tapes related to this manual and also you may contact a Kemetic priest or priestess for additional guidance. Once you are assisted through understanding the fundamental philosophy behind the Kemetic culture (MAAT) and once you work through the first principle {HONOR}, you will be better equipped to work more independently while asking for assistance.

Note on the proposals:

Keep in mind that whatever you propose for yourself you are automatically extending the courtesy of applying those rights and protections to your partner as well.

In the next pages you will write your reflections about each of the principles and any other concerns you may have. If you need additional space take any number of required additional pages as needed.

Step 1: PERSONAL NOTES-in the Notes section write your reflections such as why this item is important to you; why should it be included. If you seek counseling from a Maatian judge (priest/priestess) you may include those notes here.

Step 2: PROPOSAL STATEMENT-write down in 1-2 sentences your proposal statement. This is what you will discuss with your partner

Step 3: DISCUSSION NOTES-write down notes from your discussion. If you need time to reflect on them later do so. Then meet on this issue again and discuss further.

Step 4: FINAL AGREEMENT STATEMENT-When an agreement is reached you both will write down the same final statements in both of your guidebooks.

CHAPTER 4: WORKSHEETS to develop the principles that will go into the contract

INSTRUCTION

1-Work through the guiding questions by reading and reflecting upon them yourself first before discussing them with your prospective partner.

2-Next, determine your conclusion about the particular issue.

3-Next have the discussion with the prospective partner.

4-Then determine if you both can agree on a final statement to be included in the contract.

WORKSHEET FOR PRINCIPLE: Honoring yourself and your partner

Guiding questions: Review the guiding questions and make your notes here. If you need additional space add as many sheets as needed.

PERSONAL NOTES:

Proposal Statement:

Discussion Notes:

Final Agreement statement:

Kemetic Guide to Creating Positive Relationships and a Kemetic Marital Agreement

WORKSHEET FOR PRINCIPLE: Religion

Guiding questions: Review the guiding questions and make your notes here. If you need additional space add as many sheets as needed.

PERSONAL NOTES:

Proposal Statement:

Discussion Notes:

Final Agreement statement:

WORKSHEET FOR PRINCIPLE: Finances

Guiding questions: Review the guiding questions and make your notes here. If you need additional space add as many sheets as needed.

PERSONAL NOTES:

Proposal Statement:

Discussion Notes:

Final Agreement statement:

WORKSHEET FOR PRINCIPLE: Sex

Guiding questions: Review the guiding questions and make your notes here. If you need additional space add as many sheets as needed.

PERSONAL NOTES:

Proposal Statement:

Discussion Notes:

Final Agreement statement:

WORKSHEET FOR PRINCIPLE: Progeny

Guiding questions: Review the guiding questions and make your notes here. If you need additional space add as many sheets as needed.

PERSONAL NOTES:

Proposal Statement:

Discussion Notes:

Final Agreement statement:

WORKSHEET FOR PRINCIPLE: Health

Guiding questions: Review the guiding questions and make your notes here. If you need additional space add as many sheets as needed.

PERSONAL NOTES:

Proposal Statement:

Discussion Notes:

Final Agreement statement:

WORKSHEET FOR PRINCIPLE: Chores and Family responsibilities

Guiding questions: Review the guiding questions and make your notes here. If you need additional space add as many sheets as needed.

PERSONAL NOTES:

Proposal Statement:

Discussion Notes:

Final Agreement statement:

WORKSHEET FOR PRINCIPLE: Divorce

Guiding questions: Review the guiding questions and make your notes here. If you need additional space add as many sheets as needed.

PERSONAL NOTES:

Proposal Statement:

Discussion Notes:

Final Agreement statement:

WORKSHEET FOR PRINCIPLE: *Death*

Guiding questions: Review the guiding questions and make your notes here. If you need additional space add as many sheets as needed.

PERSONAL NOTES:

Proposal Statement:

Discussion Notes:

Final Agreement statement:

WORKSHEET FOR PRINCIPLE: Other_____

Guiding questions: Use this section for your personal principles if any.

PERSONAL NOTES:

Proposal Statement:

Discussion Notes:

Final Agreement statement:

WORKSHEET FOR PRINCIPLE: Other_____

Guiding questions: Use this section for your personal principles if any.

PERSONAL NOTES:

Proposal Statement:

Discussion Notes:

Final Agreement statement:

CHAPTER 5: PUTTING THE FINAL STATEMENTS INTO THE FINAL MARITAL AGREEMENT/CONTRACT DOCUMENT

The final marital agreement or contract will have the following items:

It contained:

- The date
- The contractors (future wife and husband)
- The names of both sets of parents
- Wife's profession
- Husband's profession
- The scribe who drew up the contract
- The names of the witnesses
- The details of the settlement
    - This is the listing of the <u>Final Agreement statements</u> that are agreed to by both marital partners.

The finished document is to be given to a third party for safekeeping or kept among the records of the local temple or courthouse.

Samples Kemetic Marriage Contracts

The following sample contains some parameters arrived at by two fictitious individuals. Your contract may contain similar or other parameters and can be as long or short as you desire. The following has been included to give an idea of how a final Kemetic Marriage Contract might look after engaging in the process outlined in this book. The first sample is from an ancient marriage contract and the second is a modern production based on similar principles but taking into account present day realities and issues.

ANCIENT EGYPTIAN MARRIAGE CONTRACT / AGREEMENT

Here's a standard marriage contract that was found among the numerous records left by the ancient Egyptians. It contained:

The date (the year of the reign of the ruling monarch)
The contractors (future husband and wife)
The names of both sets of parents
Husband's profession (wife's rarely mentioned)
The scribe who drew up the contract
The names of the witnesses

Then the details of the settlement followed. Here is the beginning of a marriage contract from 219 BC:

"The Blemmyann, born in Egypt, son of Horpais, whose mother is Wenis, has said to the woman Tais, daughter of the Khahor, whose mother is Tairerdjeret: I have made you a married woman. As your woman's portion, I give you two pieces of silver...If I dismiss you as wife and dislike you and prefer another woman to you as wife, I will give you two pieces of silver in addition to the two pieces of silver mentioned above...and I will give you one third of each and everything that will accrue to you and me."

It is Agreed, For the Purpose of Entering Into A Kemetic Marriage Between

Partner #1 _____ and Partner #2 _____

General Framework of Agreement:

Both individual signatories to this document agree to uphold the following parameters set forth by each as guidelines for governing their marital partnership. These may be amended by mutual agreement. The Honor and other principles (besides the Maatian and non-negotiable principles) set forth in this contract are pledges by each partner in this agreement and are understood as good faith contractual obligations by each partner, to be upheld, to the best of their abilities and to the minimal satisfaction of their partner. The inability or unwillingness to make such effort may be deemed as sufficient cause for seeking redress of the issues (such as marital counseling), or if this cannot resolve the issue(s), dissolution may be deemed necessary by the aggrieved party. The lack of observance of any of the 42 Precepts Maat or the agreed upon Non-negotiable personal principles may be just cause for immediate dissolution of this contract or for action to repair the lack, as deemed necessary by the aggrieved party.

The agreement may be ended by either party at any time and for any reason; however, if the reason is not due to an aggrieved condition based on the parameters set forth above, the party choosing to end the agreement is responsible to leave sufficient wealth that was acquired mutually, to the party not initiating the divorce proceedings. If the dissolution of this contract is caused by the violation of either one of the 42 Precepts Maat or the agreed upon Non-negotiable personal principles the same remedy will be applied.

==============

CLAUSES CREATED BY PATNER #1

Partner #1- Non-Negotiable Principles

- Non-violence in dealing with child(ren) (No spanking)

- Weekly relationship communication meetings –

- Integrative Medicine – Alternative medicine given priority

- Foster spiritual practices once per week as a family

- Do not want to be hungry, homeless or poor – to maintain a level of food and shelter (safety net) – putting away 10% of income monthly until get to the point of having a funds available to support the family for 1 year at a stable level before venturing into other opportunities.

- Consultation for any major financial decisions (over $200).

- Not allowing a break off of communication for more than 48 hours. If someone does not want to address an issue at the moment, they can call a time out for up to 48 hours, and within that time frame of 48 hours, that person would need to reschedule a time to meet.

Partner #1- Principles To Honor Partner #1's Soul:

- Affections-I would feel honored when my partner touches me in a non-sexual manner on a regular basis (hugging, holding hands, rubbing my back – especially when I have had a hard day, kissing).

- More coordination on doing home maintenance things as a family unit; e.g., home activities such as cleanup, etc. Both parties participate in cleaning (take out garbage, do not eat in the bedroom, clean car); perform such duties as a family.

- Do at least one annual Family tradition for example, Kwanza in the home and community.

- Accountability for what both partner's say and follow up. Inform partner when individual plans change.

Partner #1's Principles to Honor Partner #2's Soul:

- I will strive to not to speak stridently (high pitched and loud) or with disrespect to my partner when some stressful issue arises between us or in our individual lives.

- I will strive to respect my partner's time and space and work to have patience when my partner is engaged in project or working.

- I will strive to participate more in community activities that my partner is engaged in because I recognize that this is something that is important to him.

- I will strive to be more proactive in reminding my partner of my important needs, in general but also during the weekly meetings as I recognize that he may be engaged in work and would appreciate my reminding him.

CLAUSES CREATED BY PATNER #2

Partner #2's Non – Negotiable Principles

- Live the Kemetic (secular/Maatian) and Neterian (spiritual) lifestyle.

- Veganism family diet – We agree to have a vegan diet for ourselves and our children. Veganism means no meat of any kind, no dairy of any kind, and with respect to honey and other animal products such as leather, drum skins, to try to find alternatives and avoid as much as possible.

- Dedicate life to -Working towards Community Building within the African Community and to have my partner support me in this journey as much as possible.

- Support family and community to have a viable environment for our children to grow in.

Partner #2's Principles To Honor Partner #2's Soul

- I will strive to treat my partner with warmth, diplomacy, patience, and respect to honor the divine presence within me.

Partner #2's Principles To Honor Partner #1's Soul

- I will strive to honor my partner as Un Nefer a divine being reflected in me

- I will nurture **Partner #1's**, realizing that **Partner #1's** is the nurturer in me.

Partner #1 and Partner #2 Mutual Agreements

- ❖ By signing this contract for marriage based on ancient Kemetic principles we both agree that if there should come a time to separate that we will do so protecting the honor, integrity, and financial well-being of each other.

- ❖ We will honor the spirit of this contract, to be reasonable in its interpretation and not contend in the courts or legal system.

- ❖ If we need advice on any parameter of this contract we will seek the advice of a qualified Kemetic Wisdom practitioner and then come to a mutual agreement thereby.

- ❖ We agree to divide any assets developed together during the period of the marriage.

- ❖ If we produced any children we agree that we will both protect their honor, well-being and financial support during or after the marriage and unless there is violation of parameters of the contract or a violation of the trust of the child(ren) that there will be no obstruction to equal time spent with both parents after the marriage.

- ❖ We both agree to agree first before becoming pregnant and having children.

- ❖ We both agree to consult each other on any major financial activities that are above the amount of $_____.

_____   _____
Partner #1   **Date**   **Witness**
_____   _____
Partner #2   **Date**   **Witness**

INDEX

Absolute, 87
Africa, 34, 94, 103, 105, 107, 108
African Proverbial Wisdom Teachings, 115
African Religion, 87, 96, 97, 102
Allopathic, 87
Amenta, 95
Amentet, 97
American Heritage Dictionary, Dictionary, 102
American Theocracy, 106
Ancient Egypt, 10, 11, 14, 15, 16, 17, 18, 19, 20, 21, 22, 26, 28, 30, 87, 88, 89, 90, 91, 92, 93, 94, 95, 96, 97, 98, 99, 100, 101, 102, 103, 104, 105, 107, 108, 112, 113, 114, 116
Ancient Egyptian Wisdom Texts, 11, 114
anger, 100
Ani, 19
Anu, 96
Anu (Greek Heliopolis), 96
Anunian Theology, 97
Ari, 24
Aryan, 89
Asar, 94, 95, 98, 99
Asar and Aset, 94
Asarian Resurrection, 94, 98, 99, 100, 103
Aset, 17, 90, 94, 95, 97, 98, 99
Aset (Isis), 17, 90, 94, 95, 97, 98, 99
Ashanti, 115
Asia, 108
Asia Minor, 108
Asiatic, 105, 107, 108
Assyrians, 113
Astral, 95
Astral Plane, 95
Atlantis, 104
Awakening, 95
Balance, 30
Balance of Mind, 30
Being, 37, 97
Bhagavad Gita, 113
Bible, 98
Black, 108
Black XE "Black" Africa, 108
Book of Coming Forth By Day, 95, 96
Book of Enlightenment, 17

Book of the Dead, see also Rau Nu Prt M Hru, 17, 96, 114
brown, 26
Buddha, 103, 105
Buddhism, 97, 105
Buddhist, 94, 105
Catholic, 14, 98
Catholic Church, 98
Child, 99
Christ, 95
Christianity, 14, 86, 97, 98
Church, 98
Civilization, 89, 90, 105, 106, 107, 108
coercion, 106
Collapse, 106
color, 26, 111, 114
Color, 111
Conflict, 34, 106, 115
Conscience, 30
Consciousness, 3, 94, 114
Consciousness, human, 87
Coptic, 95
cosmic force, 17, 98, 104
Creation, 94, 96, 97, 114
Culture, 10, 93, 104, 110
Death, 46, 69, 106
December, 98
delusion, 16
Demotic, 28
Denderah, 95
Desire, 115
Devotional Love, 91
Diet, 88
Duat, 95
Edfu, 95
Egyptian Book of Coming Forth By Day, 95
Egyptian Mysteries, 15, 17, 88, 100, 101, 116
Egyptian Physics, 97
Egyptian Proverb, 91
EGYPTIAN PROVERBS, 91
Egyptian Yoga, 86, 88, 94, 95, 96
Egyptian Yoga see also Kamitan Yoga, 37, 86, 87, 88, 94, 95, 96
Egyptologists, 102, 112
Empire culture, 106

Enlightenment, 3, 30, 37, 87, 88, 90, 92, 94, 97, 98, 100, 105, 115
Ethics, 10, 88, 89, 105, 107, 108, 115
Ethiopia, 115
Eucharist, 95
evil, 99, 102
Evil, 103
Exercise, 94
Faith, 109
faith-based, 21
Feelings, 34
Finances, 44, 57
Galla, 115
Galla culture, 115
Geb, 94
Ghana, 115
global economy, 106
Globalization, 106
God, 14, 15, 90, 91, 96, 97, 103, 111
Goddess, 97, 111
Goddesses, 94, 102
Gods, 94, 102
gods and goddesses, 15, 97, 102, 104
Good, 103
Gospels, 98
Greece, 88, 104
Greek philosophy, 86
Greeks, 113
Hate, 115
Hatha Yoga, 107
Hathor, 94, 95, 97, 100
Hatred, 115
Health, 46, 63, 87, 97
HEART, 99, 109
HEART (ALSO SEE AB, MIND, CONSCIENCE), 99, 109
Heaven, 98
Heru, 17, 18, 95, 96, 98, 99, 103, 114
Heru (see Horus), 17, 18, 95, 96, 98, 99, 103, 114
Hetheru, 100
Hetheru (Hetheru, Hathor), 100
Hieroglyphic, 92, 112
Hieroglyphic Writing, language, 92, 112
Hinduism, 97
Hindus, 37, 101
Honesty, 30
hope, 49, 110, 112
Humanity, 30, 101
Iamblichus, 113

India, 88, 89, 90, 92, 94, 105, 107
Indian Yoga, 89
Indus, 89
Indus Valley, 89
Initiate, 88
Isis, 90, 94, 95, 98
Isis, See also Aset, 90, 94, 95, 98
Islam, 86
Jesus, 14, 95, 98, 99
Jesus Christ, 95
Judaism, 86
Kabbalah, 86
Kamit (Egypt), 102
Kamitan, 88, 104
Karma, 37, 92
Kemetic, 2, 10, 13, 15, 18, 22, 24, 25, 26, 28, 29, 30, 34, 39, 40, 41, 43, 46, 49, 50, 75, 77, 78, 105, 109
Khemn, see also ignorance, 102
King, 99, 103
Kingdom, 98
Kingdom of Heaven, 98
KMT (Ancient Egypt). See also Kamit, 43
Krishna, 99
Life, 93, 103, 109, 111, 114
Life Force, 93
Love, 91
Maat, 10, 11, 15, 20, 29, 30, 34, 40, 43, 50, 77, 92, 97, 99, 104, 109, 114, 116
MAAT, 91
Maat Philosophy, 11, 30, 99, 104, 109
MAATI, 3, 92
Malawi, 115
Matter, 97
media, 106
Meditation, 88, 91, 93
Medu Neter, 101
Memphite Theology, 97
Meskhenet, 92
Metaphysics, 97, 114
Middle East, 86
Min, 94
Mind, 30
Music, 32, 112
Mysteries, 88, 100, 101, 113, 116
mystical philosophy, 15, 105, 114
Mysticism, 89, 90, 96, 97, 100, 105, 107, 108
Neberdjer, 87
Nefer, 78
Nehast, 37, 102

neo-con, 106
Neter, 43, 91, 95, 101, 102, 105, 112, 116
Neterian, 15, 78, 102, 105
Neteru, 102
New Age, 10
Nigeria, 115
Non-violence, 30, 77
Nut, 94
Orion Star Constellation, 98
Orthodox, 14, 101
Osiris, 94, 95, 103
Peace, 115
Peace (see also Hetep), 115
Persians, 113
PERT EM HERU, SEE ALSO BOOK OF THE DEAD, 96
Philae, 95
Philosophy, 10, 30, 37, 87, 88, 89, 90, 91, 96, 97, 99, 104, 105, 107, 108, 109
pressure, 16
priests and priestesses, 94, 102
Priests and Priestesses, 88, 102
Proverbial Wisdom, 115
Psychology, 97
Ptah, 97
Queen, 103
Ra, 94
racism, 116
Racism, 115
Realization, 90
Relationships, 2, 10, 29
Religion, 15, 43, 55, 87, 89, 90, 95, 96, 97, 99, 102, 103, 104, 105, 107, 108
Resurrection, 94, 95, 97, 98, 99, 100, 103
Right Thinking, 30
Right Worship, 30
RITUAL, 100
Rituals, 97
Roman, 14, 113
Romans, 113
Rome, 104
Sages, 87, 95, 96, 100, 104
Saints, 96
Sebai, 1, 2, 29, 105, 111
See also Ra-Hrakti, 94
Self (see Ba, soul, Spirit, Universal, Ba, Neter, Heru)., 30, 34, 89, 90, 92, 95, 101, 111
Self-created lifestyle, lifestyle, 32, 46, 78
Selfless Service, 30
Sema, 2, 103, 116

Set, 103
Seti I, 93
Sex, 3, 30, 43, 59, 94
sexism, 116
Sexism, 115
Sex-Sublimation, 30
Sexuality, 11
Shedy, 88
Shetaut Neter, 15, 43, 95, 101, 102, 105, 116
Shetaut Neter See also Egyptian Religion, 15, 43, 95, 101, 102, 105, 116
Sirius, 98
skin, 26
slavery, 102
society, 11, 14, 16, 20, 22, 24, 29, 87, 102, 104, 110, 115
Soul, 78, 103
Spirit, 37
Spiritual discipline, 88
SPIRITUALITY, 88, 109
Sublimation, 3, 30, 94
Superpower, 106
Superpower Syndrome, 106
Superpower Syndrome Mandatory Conflict Complex, 106
Supreme Being, 97
TANTRA, 3, 94
TANTRA YOGA, 3, 94
Tantric Yoga, 11
Taoism, 86
Temple, 95, 100
Temple of Aset, 95
The Absolute, 87
The Black, 108
The God, 94
The Gods, 94
Theban Theology, 87
Thebes, 87, 93
Theocracy, 106
Theology, 87, 97
time and space, 20, 37, 78, 102
Tomb, 93
Tomb of Seti I, 93
transcendental reality, 102
Tree, 114
Tree of Life, 114
Triad, 87
Trinity, 95
Truth, 30
Understanding, 102

United States of America, 106
Universal Consciousness, 3, 94
Upanishads, 96, 113
USA, West, 32
Vedic, 89
Violence, 115
Waset, 87
Will, 32, 43, 44, 46
Wisdom, 10, 78, 91, 93, 113, 114, 115
Wisdom (also see Djehuti, Aset), 10, 78, 91, 93, 113, 114, 115
Witness, 78
World War II, 106
Yoga, 2, 3, 37, 86, 87, 88, 89, 90, 94, 95, 96, 97, 99, 103, 105, 107, 108
Yogic, 107, 116
Yoruba, 115

Other Books From C M Books
P.O.Box 570459
Miami, Florida, 33257
(305) 378-6253 Fax: (305) 378-6253

Prices subject to change.

1. *EGYPTIAN YOGA: THE PHILOSOPHY OF ENLIGHTENMENT* An original, fully illustrated work, including hieroglyphs, detailing the meaning of the Egyptian mysteries, tantric yoga, psycho-spiritual and physical exercises. Egyptian Yoga is a guide to the practice of the highest spiritual philosophy which leads to absolute freedom from human misery and to immortality. It is well known by scholars that Egyptian philosophy is the basis of Western and Middle Eastern religious philosophies such as *Christianity, Islam, Judaism,* the *Kabala*, and Greek philosophy, but what about Indian philosophy, Yoga and Taoism? What were the original teachings? How can they be practiced today? What is the source of pain and suffering in the world and what is the solution? Discover the deepest mysteries of the mind and universe within and outside of your self. 8.5" X 11" ISBN: 1-884564-01-1 Soft $19.95

Guide to Creating a Kemetic Marital Agreement

2. *EGYPTIAN YOGA: African Religion Volume 2-* Theban Theology U.S. In this long awaited sequel to *Egyptian Yoga: The Philosophy of Enlightenment* you will take a fascinating and enlightening journey back in time and discover the teachings which constituted the epitome of Ancient Egyptian spiritual wisdom. What are the disciplines which lead to the fulfillment of all desires? Delve into the three states of consciousness (waking, dream and deep sleep) and the fourth state which transcends them all, Neberdjer, "The Absolute." These teachings of the city of Waset (Thebes) were the crowning achievement of the Sages of Ancient Egypt. They establish the standard mystical keys for understanding the profound mystical symbolism of the Triad of human consciousness. ISBN 1-884564-39-9 $23.95

3. *THE KEMETIC DIET: GUIDE TO HEALTH, DIET AND FASTING* Health issues have always been important to human beings since the beginning of time. The earliest records of history show that the art of healing was held in high esteem since the time of Ancient Egypt. In the early 20th century, medical doctors had almost attained the status of sainthood by the promotion of the idea that they alone were "scientists" while other healing modalities and traditional healers who did not follow the "scientific method' were nothing but superstitious, ignorant charlatans who at best would take the money of their clients and at worst kill them with the unscientific "snake oils" and "irrational theories". In the late 20th century, the failure of the modern medical establishment's ability to lead the general public to good health, promoted the move by many in society towards "alternative medicine". Alternative medicine disciplines are those healing modalities which do not adhere to the philosophy of allopathic medicine. Allopathic medicine is what medical doctors practice by an large. It is the theory that disease is caused by agencies outside the body such as bacteria, viruses or physical means which affect the body. These can therefore be treated by medicines and therapies The natural healing method began in the absence of extensive technologies with the idea that all the answers for health may be found in nature or rather, the deviation from nature. Therefore, the health of the body can be restored by correcting the aberration and thereby restoring balance. This is the area that will be covered in this volume. Allopathic techniques have their place in the art of healing. However, we should not forget that the body is a grand achievement of the spirit and built into it is the capacity to maintain itself and heal itself. Ashby, Muata ISBN: 1-884564-49-6 $28.95

4. *INITIATION INTO EGYPTIAN YOGA* Shedy: Spiritual discipline or program, to go deeply into the mysteries, to study the mystery teachings and literature profoundly, to penetrate the mysteries. You will learn about the mysteries of initiation into the teachings and practice of Yoga and how to become an Initiate of the mystical sciences. This insightful manual is the first in a series which introduces you to the goals of daily spiritual and yoga practices: Meditation, Diet, Words of Power and the ancient wisdom teachings. 8.5" X 11" ISBN 1-884564-02-X   Soft Cover $24.95 U.S.

5. *THE AFRICAN ORIGINS OF CIVILIZATION, RELIGION AND YOGA SPIRITUALITY AND ETHICS PHILOSOPHY* HARD COVER EDITION Part 1, Part 2, Part 3 in one volume 683 Pages Hard Cover First Edition Three volumes in one. Over the past several years I have been asked to put together in one volume the most important evidences showing the correlations and common teachings between Kamitan (Ancient Egyptian) culture and religion and that of India. The questions of the history of Ancient Egypt, and the latest archeological evidences showing civilization and culture in Ancient Egypt and its spread to other countries, has intrigued many scholars as well as mystics over the years. Also, the possibility that Ancient Egyptian Priests and Priestesses migrated to Greece, India and other countries to carry on the traditions of the Ancient Egyptian Mysteries, has been speculated over the years as well. In chapter 1 of the book *Egyptian Yoga The Philosophy of Enlightenment,* 1995, I first introduced the deepest comparison between Ancient Egypt and India that had been brought forth up to that time. Now, in the year 2001 this new book, *THE AFRICAN ORIGINS OF CIVILIZATION, MYSTICAL RELIGION AND YOGA PHILOSOPHY,* more fully explores the motifs, symbols and philosophical correlations between Ancient Egyptian and Indian mysticism and clearly shows not only that Ancient Egypt and India were connected culturally but also

spiritually. How does this knowledge help the spiritual aspirant? This discovery has great importance for the Yogis and mystics who follow the philosophy of Ancient Egypt and the mysticism of India. It means that India has a longer history and heritage than was previously understood. It shows that the mysteries of Ancient Egypt were essentially a yoga tradition which did not die but rather developed into the modern day systems of Yoga technology of India. It further shows that African culture developed Yoga Mysticism earlier than any other civilization in history. All of this expands our understanding of the unity of culture and the deep legacy of Yoga, which stretches into the distant past, beyond the Indus Valley civilization, the earliest known high culture in India as well as the Vedic tradition of Aryan culture. Therefore, Yoga culture and mysticism is the oldest known tradition of spiritual development and Indian mysticism is an extension of the Ancient Egyptian mysticism. By understanding the legacy which Ancient Egypt gave to India the mysticism of India is better understood and by comprehending the heritage of Indian Yoga, which is rooted in Ancient Egypt the Mysticism of Ancient Egypt is also better understood. This expanded understanding allows us to prove the underlying kinship of humanity, through the common symbols, motifs and philosophies which are not disparate and confusing teachings but in reality expressions of the same study of truth through metaphysics and mystical realization of Self. (HARD COVER) ISBN: 1-884564-50-X $45.00 U.S.   8 1/2" X 11"

6. *AFRICAN ORIGINS BOOK 1 PART 1* African Origins of African Civilization, Religion, Yoga Mysticism and Ethics Philosophy-Soft Cover $24.95 ISBN: 1-884564-55-0

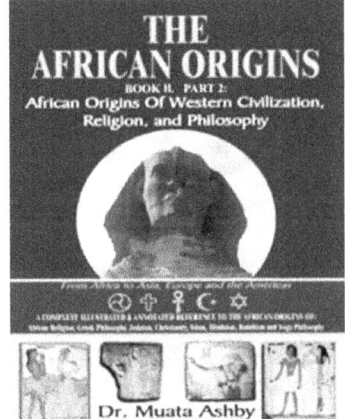

7. *AFRICAN ORIGINS BOOK 2 PART 2* African Origins of Western Civilization, Religion and Philosophy (Soft) -Soft Cover $24.95 ISBN: 1-884564-56-9

Guide to Creating a Kemetic Marital Agreement

8. *EGYPT AND INDIA AFRICAN ORIGINS OF Eastern Civilization, Religion, Yoga Mysticism and Philosophy-* Soft Cover $29.95 (Soft) ISBN: 1-884564-57-7

9. *THE MYSTERIES OF ISIS:* **The Ancient Egyptian Philosophy of Self-Realization** - There are several paths to discover the Divine and the mysteries of the higher Self. This volume details the mystery teachings of the goddess Aset (Isis) from Ancient Egypt- the path of wisdom. It includes the teachings of her temple and the disciplines that are enjoined for the initiates of the temple of Aset as they were given in ancient times. Also, this book includes the teachings of the main myths of Aset that lead a human being to spiritual enlightenment and immortality. Through the study of ancient myth and the illumination of initiatic understanding the idea of God is expanded from the mythological comprehension to the metaphysical. Then this metaphysical understanding is related to you, the student, so as to begin understanding your true divine nature. ISBN 1-884564-24-0 $22.99

10. *EGYPTIAN PROVERBS:* collection of —Ancient Egyptian Proverbs and Wisdom Teachings -How to live according to MAAT Philosophy. Beginning Meditation. All proverbs are indexed for easy searches. For the first time in one volume, ——Ancient Egyptian Proverbs, wisdom teachings and meditations, fully illustrated with hieroglyphic text and symbols. EGYPTIAN PROVERBS is a unique collection of knowledge and wisdom which you can put into practice today and transform your life. $14.95 U.S ISBN: 1-884564-00-3

11. *GOD OF LOVE: THE PATH OF DIVINE LOVE The Process of Mystical Transformation and The Path of Divine Love* This Volume focuses on the ancient wisdom teachings of "Neter Merri" –the Ancient Egyptian philosophy of Divine Love and how to use them in a scientific process for self-transformation. Love is one of the most powerful human emotions. It is also the source of Divine feeling that unifies God and the individual human being. When love is fragmented and diminished by egoism the Divine connection is lost. The Ancient tradition of Neter Merri leads human beings back to their Divine connection, allowing them to discover their innate glorious self that is actually Divine and immortal. This volume will detail the process of transformation from ordinary consciousness to cosmic consciousness through the integrated practice of the teachings and the path of Devotional Love toward the Divine. 5.5"x 8.5" ISBN 1-884564-11-9 $22.95

12. *INTRODUCTION TO MAAT PHILOSOPHY: Spiritual Enlightenment Through the Path of Virtue*   Known commonly as Karma in India, the teachings of MAAT contain an extensive philosophy based on ariu (deeds) and their fructification in the form of shai and renenet (fortune and destiny, leading to Meskhenet (fate in a future birth) for living virtuously and with orderly wisdom are explained and the student is to begin practicing the precepts of Maat in daily life so as to promote the process of purification of the heart in preparation for the judgment of the soul. This judgment will be understood not as an event that will occur at the time of death but as an event that occurs continuously, at every moment in the life of the individual. The student will learn how to become allied with the forces of the Higher Self and to thereby begin cleansing the mind (heart) of impurities so as to attain a higher vision of reality. ISBN 1-884564-20-8 $22.99

13. *MEDITATION The Ancient Egyptian Path to Enlightenment*   Many people do not know about the rich history of meditation practice in Ancient Egypt. This volume outlines the theory of meditation and presents the Ancient Egyptian Hieroglyphic text which give instruction as to the nature of the mind and its three modes of expression. It also presents the texts which give instruction on the practice of meditation for spiritual Enlightenment and unity with the Divine. This volume allows the reader to begin practicing meditation by explaining, in easy to understand terms, the simplest form of meditation and working up to the most advanced form which was practiced in ancient times and which is still practiced by yogis around the world in modern times. ISBN 1-884564-27-7 $22.99

14. *THE GLORIOUS LIGHT MEDITATION* TECHNIQUE OF ANCIENT EGYPT New for the year 2000. This volume is based on the earliest known instruction in history given for the practice of formal meditation. Discovered by Dr. Muata Ashby, it is inscribed on the walls of the Tomb of Seti I in Thebes Egypt. This volume details the philosophy and practice of this unique system of meditation originated in Ancient Egypt and the earliest practice of meditation known in the world which occurred in the most advanced African Culture. ISBN: 1-884564-15-1 $16.95 (PB)

15. *THE SERPENT POWER: The Ancient Egyptian Mystical Wisdom of the Inner Life Force.* This Volume specifically deals with the latent life Force energy of the universe and in the human body, its control and sublimation. How to develop the Life Force energy of the subtle body. This Volume will introduce the esoteric wisdom of the science of how virtuous living acts in a subtle and mysterious way to cleanse the latent psychic energy conduits and vortices of the spiritual body. ISBN 1-884564-19-4 $22.95

Guide to Creating a Kemetic Marital Agreement

16. *EGYPTIAN YOGA The Postures of The Gods and Goddesses* Discover the physical postures and exercises practiced thousands of years ago in Ancient Egypt which are today known as Yoga exercises. Discover the history of the postures and how they were transferred from Ancient Egypt in Africa to India through Buddhist Tantrism. Then practice the postures as you discover the mythic teaching that originally gave birth to the postures and was practiced by the Ancient Egyptian priests and priestesses. This work is based on the pictures and teachings from the Creation story of Ra, The Asarian Resurrection Myth and the carvings and reliefs from various Temples in Ancient Egypt 8.5" X 11" ISBN 1-884564-10-0 Soft Cover $21.95   Exercise video $20

17. *SACRED SEXUALITY: ANCIENT EGYPTIAN TANTRA YOGA: The Art of Sex* Sublimation and Universal Consciousness This Volume will expand on the male and female principles within the human body and in the universe and further detail the sublimation of sexual energy into spiritual energy. The student will study the deities Min and Hathor, Asar and Aset, Geb and Nut and discover the mystical implications for a practical spiritual discipline. This Volume will also focus on the Tantric aspects of Ancient Egyptian and Indian mysticism, the purpose of sex and the mystical teachings of sexual sublimation which lead to self-knowledge and Enlightenment. ISBN 1-884564-03-8 $24.95

18. *AFRICAN RELIGION Volume 4: ASARIAN THEOLOGY: RESURRECTING OSIRIS* The path of Mystical Awakening and the Keys to Immortality NEW REVISED AND EXPANDED EDITION! The Ancient Sages created stories based on human and superhuman beings whose struggles, aspirations, needs and desires ultimately lead them to discover their true Self. The myth of Aset, Asar and Heru is no exception in this area. While there is no one source where the entire story may be found, pieces of it are inscribed in various ancient Temples walls, tombs, steles and papyri. For the first time available, the complete myth of Asar, Aset and Heru has been compiled from original Ancient Egyptian, Greek and Coptic Texts. This epic myth has been richly illustrated with reliefs from the Temple of Heru at Edfu, the Temple of Aset at Philae, the Temple of Asar at Abydos, the Temple of Hathor at Denderah and various papyri, inscriptions and reliefs. Discover the myth which inspired the teachings of the *Shetaut Neter* (Egyptian Mystery System - Egyptian Yoga) and the Egyptian Book of Coming Forth By Day. Also, discover the three levels of Ancient Egyptian Religion, how to understand the mysteries of the Duat or Astral World and how to discover the abode of the Supreme in the Amenta, *The Other World* The ancient religion of Asar, Aset and Heru, if properly understood, contains all of the elements necessary to lead the sincere aspirant to attain immortality through inner self-discovery. This volume presents the entire myth and explores the main mystical themes and rituals associated with the myth for understating human existence, creation and the way to achieve spiritual emancipation - *Resurrection.* The Asarian myth is so powerful that it influenced and is still having an effect on the major world religions. Discover the origins and mystical meaning of the Christian Trinity, the Eucharist ritual and the ancient origin of the birthday of Jesus Christ. Soft Cover ISBN: 1-884564-27-5 $24.95

19. *THE EGYPTIAN BOOK OF THE DEAD MYSTICISM OF THE PERT EM HERU* " I Know myself, I know myself, I am One With God!–From the Pert Em Heru "The Ru Pert em Heru" or "Ancient Egyptian Book of The Dead," or "Book of Coming Forth By Day" as it is more popularly known, has fascinated the world since the successful translation of Ancient Egyptian hieroglyphic scripture over 150 years ago. The astonishing writings in it reveal that the Ancient Egyptians believed in life after death and in an ultimate destiny to discover the Divine. The elegance and aesthetic beauty of the hieroglyphic text itself has inspired many see it as an art form in and of itself. But is there more to it than that? Did the Ancient Egyptian wisdom contain more than just aphorisms and hopes of eternal life beyond death? In this volume Dr. Muata Ashby, the author of over 25 books on Ancient Egyptian Yoga Philosophy has produced a new translation of the original texts which uncovers a mystical teaching underlying the sayings and rituals instituted by the Ancient Egyptian Sages and Saints. "Once the philosophy of Ancient Egypt is understood as a mystical tradition instead of as a religion or primitive mythology, it reveals its secrets which if practiced today will lead anyone to discover the glory of spiritual self-discovery. The Pert em Heru is in every way comparable to the Indian Upanishads or the Tibetan Book of the Dead." $28.95   ISBN# 1-884564-28-3 Size: 8½" X 11

20. *African Religion VOL. 1- ANUNIAN THEOLOGY THE MYSTERIES OF RA* The Philosophy of Anu and The Mystical Teachings of The Ancient Egyptian Creation Myth Discover the mystical teachings

contained in the Creation Myth and the gods and goddesses who brought creation and human beings into existence. The Creation myth of Anu is the source of Anunian Theology but also of the other main theological systems of Ancient Egypt that also influenced other world religions including Christianity, Hinduism and Buddhism. The Creation Myth holds the key to understanding the universe and for attaining spiritual Enlightenment. ISBN: 1-884564-38-0 $19.95

21. *African Religion VOL 3: Memphite Theology: MYSTERIES OF MIND* Mystical Psychology & Mental Health for Enlightenment and Immortality based on the Ancient Egyptian Philosophy of Menefer - Mysticism of Ptah, Egyptian Physics and Yoga Metaphysics and the Hidden properties of Matter. This volume uncovers the mystical psychology of the Ancient Egyptian wisdom teachings centering on the philosophy of the Ancient Egyptian city of Menefer (Memphite Theology). How to understand the mind and how to control the senses and lead the mind to health, clarity and mystical self-discovery. This Volume will also go deeper into the philosophy of God as creation and will explore the concepts of modern science and how they correlate with ancient teachings. This Volume will lay the ground work for the understanding of the philosophy of universal consciousness and the initiatic/yogic insight into who or what is God? ISBN 1-884564-07-0 $22.95

22. AFRICAN RELIGION VOLUME 5: THE GODDESS AND THE EGYPTIAN MYSTERIESTHE PATH OF THE GODDESS THE GODDESS PATH The Secret Forms of the Goddess and the Rituals of Resurrection The Supreme Being may be worshipped as father or as mother. *Ushet Rekhat* or *Mother Worship*, is the spiritual process of worshipping the Divine in the form of the Divine Goddess. It celebrates the most important forms of the Goddess including *Nathor, Maat, Aset, Arat, Amentet and Hathor* and explores their

Guide to Creating a Kemetic Marital Agreement

mystical meaning as well as the rising of *Sirius,* the star of Aset (Aset) and the new birth of Hor (Heru). The end of the year is a time of reckoning, reflection and engendering a new or renewed positive movement toward attaining spiritual Enlightenment. The Mother Worship devotional meditation ritual, performed on five days during the month of December and on New Year's Eve, is based on the Ushet Rekhit. During the ceremony, the cosmic forces, symbolized by Sirius - and the constellation of Orion ---, are harnessed through the understanding and devotional attitude of the participant. This propitiation draws the light of wisdom and health to all those who share in the ritual, leading to prosperity and wisdom. $14.95 ISBN 1-884564-18-6

23. *THE MYSTICAL JOURNEY FROM JESUS TO CHRIST* Discover the ancient Egyptian origins of Christianity before the Catholic Church and learn the mystical teachings given by Jesus to assist all humanity in becoming Christlike. Discover the secret meaning of the Gospels that were discovered in Egypt. Also discover how and why so many Christian churches came into being. Discover that the Bible still holds the keys to mystical realization even though its original writings were changed by the church. Discover how to practice the original teachings of Christianity which leads to the Kingdom of Heaven. $24.95   ISBN# 1-884564-05-4 size: 8½" X 11"

24. THE STORY OF ASAR, ASET AND HERU: An Ancient Egyptian Legend (For Children)   Now for the first time, the most ancient myth of Ancient Egypt comes alive for children. Inspired by the books *The Asarian Resurrection: The Ancient Egyptian Bible* and *The Mystical Teachings of The Asarian Resurrection, The Story of Asar, Aset and Heru* is an easy to understand and thrilling tale which inspired the children of Ancient Egypt to aspire to greatness and righteousness.   If you and your child have enjoyed

stories like *The Lion King* and *Star Wars you will love The Story of Asar, Aset and Heru*. Also, if you know the story of Jesus and Krishna you will discover than Ancient Egypt had a similar myth and that this myth carries important spiritual teachings for living a fruitful and fulfilling life. This book may be used along with *The Parents Guide To The Asarian Resurrection Myth: How to Teach Yourself and Your Child the Principles of Universal Mystical Religion*. The guide provides some background to the Asarian Resurrection myth and it also gives insight into the mystical teachings contained in it which you may introduce to your child. It is designed for parents who wish to grow spiritually with their children and it serves as an introduction for those who would like to study the Asarian Resurrection Myth in depth and to practice its teachings. 8.5" X 11"   ISBN: 1-884564-31-3 $12.95

25.   *THE PARENTS GUIDE TO THE AUSARIAN RESURRECTION MYTH:* How to Teach Yourself and Your Child the Principles of Universal Mystical Religion.   This insightful manual brings for the timeless wisdom of the ancient through the Ancient Egyptian myth of Asar, Aset and Heru and the mystical teachings contained in it for parents who want to guide their children to understand and practice the teachings of mystical spirituality. This manual may be used with the children's storybook *The Story of Asar, Aset and Heru* by Dr. Muata Abhaya Ashby.   ISBN: 1-884564-30-5 $16.95

26.   *HEALING THE CRIMINAL HEART.* Introduction to Maat Philosophy, Yoga and Spiritual Redemption Through the Path of Virtue   Who is a criminal? Is there such a thing as a criminal heart? What is the source of evil and sinfulness and is there any way to rise above it? Is there redemption for those who have committed sins, even the worst crimes?   Ancient Egyptian mystical psychology holds important answers

to these questions. Over ten thousand years ago mystical psychologists, the Sages of Ancient Egypt, studied and charted the human mind and spirit and laid out a path which will lead to spiritual redemption, prosperity and Enlightenment.   This introductory volume brings forth the teachings of the Asarian Resurrection, the most important myth of Ancient Egypt, with relation to the faults of human existence: anger, hatred, greed, lust, animosity, discontent, ignorance, egoism jealousy, bitterness, and a myriad of psycho-spiritual ailments which keep a human being in a state of negativity and adversity   ISBN: 1-884564-17-8 $15.95

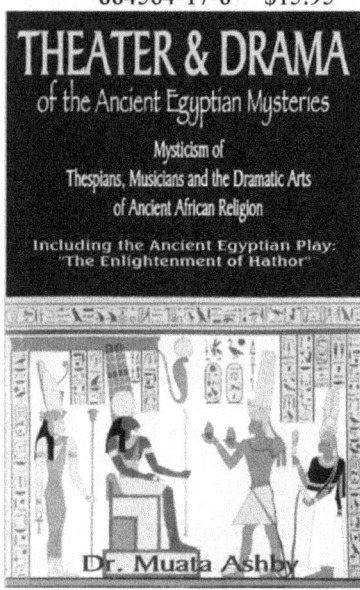

27. *TEMPLE RITUAL OF THE ANCIENT EGYPTIAN MYSTERIES--THEATER & DRAMA OF THE ANCIENT EGYPTIAN MYSTERIES*: Details the practice of the mysteries and ritual program of the temple and the philosophy an practice of the ritual of the mysteries, its purpose and execution. Featuring the Ancient Egyptian stage play-"The Enlightenment of Hathor' Based on an Ancient Egyptian Drama, The original Theater -Mysticism of the Temple of Hetheru 1-884564-14-3 $19.95   By Dr. Muata Ashby

28. *GUIDE TO PRINT ON DEMAND: SELF-PUBLISH FOR PROFIT,* SPIRITUAL FULFILLMENT AND SERVICE TO HUMANITY Everyone asks us how we produced so many books in such a short time. Here are the secrets to writing and producing books that uplift humanity and how to get them printed for a fraction of the regular cost. Anyone can become an author even if they have limited funds. All that is necessary is the willingness to learn how the printing and book business work and the desire to follow the special instructions given here for preparing your manuscript format. Then you take your work directly to the non-traditional companies who can produce your books for less than the traditional book printer can. ISBN: 1-884564-40-2 $16.95 U. S.

29. *Egyptian Mysteries: Vol. 1,* Shetaut Neter What are the Mysteries? For thousands of years the spiritual tradition of Ancient Egypt, S*hetaut Neter,* "The Egyptian Mysteries," "The Secret Teachings," have fascinated, tantalized and amazed the world. At one time exalted and recognized as the highest culture of the world, by Africans, Europeans, Asiatics, Hindus, Buddhists and other cultures of the ancient world, in time it was shunned by the emerging orthodox world religions. Its temples desecrated, its philosophy maligned, its tradition spurned, its philosophy dormant in the mystical *Medu Neter*, the mysterious

Guide to Creating a Kemetic Marital Agreement

hieroglyphic texts which hold the secret symbolic meaning that has scarcely been discerned up to now. What are the secrets of *Nehast* {spiritual awakening and emancipation, resurrection}. More than just a literal translation, this volume is for awakening to the secret code *Shetitu* of the teaching which was not deciphered by Egyptologists, nor could be understood by ordinary spiritualists. This book is a reinstatement of the original science made available for our times, to the reincarnated followers of Ancient Egyptian culture and the prospect of spiritual freedom to break the bonds of *Khemn,* "ignorance," and slavery to evil forces: *Såaa* . ISBN: 1-884564-41-0 $19.99

30. *EGYPTIAN MYSTERIES VOL 2:* Dictionary of Gods and Goddesses This book is about the mystery of neteru, the gods and goddesses of Ancient Egypt (Kamit, Kemet). Neteru means "Gods and Goddesses." But the Neterian teaching of Neteru represents more than the usual limited modern day concept of "divinities" or "spirits." The Neteru of Kamit are also metaphors, cosmic principles and vehicles for the enlightening teachings of Shetaut Neter (Ancient Egyptian-African Religion). Actually they are the elements for one of the most advanced systems of spirituality ever conceived in human history. Understanding the concept of neteru provides a firm basis for spiritual evolution and the pathway for viable culture, peace on earth and a healthy human society.   Why is it important to have gods and goddesses in our lives? In order for spiritual evolution to be possible, once a human being has accepted that there is existence after death and there is a transcendental being who exists beyond time and space knowledge, human beings need a connection to that which transcends the ordinary experience of human life in time and space and a means to understand the transcendental reality beyond the mundane reality. ISBN: 1-884564-23-2 $21.95

31. *EGYPTIAN MYSTERIES VOL. 3* The Priests and Priestesses of Ancient Egypt This volume details the path of Neterian priesthood, the joys, challenges and rewards of advanced Neterian life, the teachings that allowed the priests and priestesses to manage the most long lived civilization in human history and how that path can be adopted today; for those who want to tread the path of the Clergy of Shetaut Neter. ISBN: 1-884564-53-4 $24.95

32. *The War of Heru and Set:* The Struggle of Good and Evil for Control of the World and The Human Soul This volume contains a novelized version of the Asarian Resurrection myth that is based on the actual scriptures presented in the Book Asarian Religion (old name –Resurrecting Osiris). This volume is prepared in the form of a screenplay and can be easily adapted to be used as a stage play. Spiritual seeking is a mythic journey that has many emotional highs and lows, ecstasies and depressions, victories and frustrations. This is the War of Life that is played out in the myth as the struggle of Heru and Set and those are mythic characters that represent the human Higher and Lower self. How to understand the war and emerge victorious in the journey o life? The ultimate victory and fulfillment can be experienced, which is not changeable or lost in time. The purpose of myth is to convey the wisdom of life through the story of divinities who show the way to overcome the challenges and foibles of life. In this volume the feelings and emotions of the characters of the myth have been highlighted to show the deeply rich texture of the Ancient Egyptian myth. This myth contains deep spiritual teachings and insights into the nature of self, of God and the mysteries of life and the means to discover the true meaning of life and thereby achieve the true purpose of life. To become victorious in the battle of life means to become the King (or Queen) of Egypt.Have you seen movies like The Lion King, Hamlet, The Odyssey, or The Little Buddha? These have been some of the most popular movies in modern times. The Sema Institute of Yoga is dedicated to researching and presenting the wisdom and culture of ancient Africa. The Script is designed to be produced as a motion picture but may be addapted for the theater as well. $21.95 copyright 1998 By Dr. Muata Ashby ISBN 1-8840564-44-5

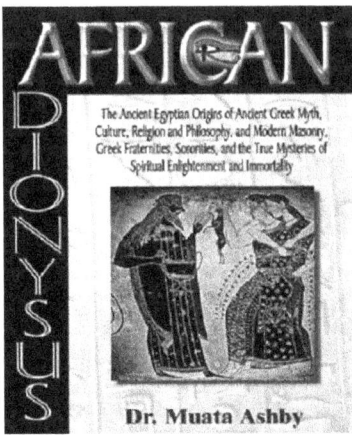

Guide to Creating a Kemetic Marital Agreement

33. *AFRICAN DIONYSUS: FROM EGYPT TO GREECE:* The Kamitan Origins of Greek Culture and Religion ISBN: 1-884564-47-X FROM EGYPT TO GREECE This insightful manual is a reference to Ancient Egyptian mythology and philosophy and its correlation to what later became known as Greek and Rome mythology and philosophy. It outlines the basic tenets of the mythologies and shoes the ancient origins of Greek culture in Ancient Egypt. This volume also documents the origins of the Greek alphabet in Egypt as well as Greek religion, myth and philosophy of the gods and goddesses from Egypt from the myth of Atlantis and archaic period with the Minoans to the Classical period. This volume also acts as a resource for Colleges students who would like to set up fraternities and sororities based on the original Ancient Egyptian principles of Sheti and Maat philosophy. ISBN: 1-884564-47-X $22.95 U.S.

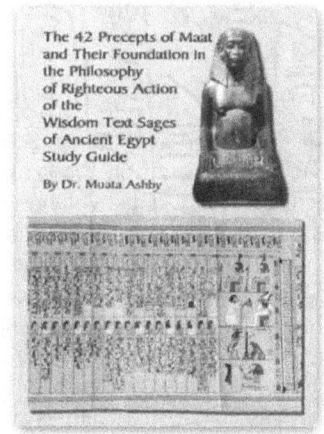

34. *THE FORTY TWO PRECEPTS OF MAAT, THE PHILOSOPHY OF RIGHTEOUS ACTION AND THE ANCIENT EGYPTIAN WISDOM TEXTS* <u>ADVANCED STUDIES</u> This manual is designed for use with the 1998 Maat Philosophy Class conducted by Dr. Muata Ashby. This is a detailed study of Maat Philosophy. It contains a compilation of the 42 laws or precepts of Maat and the corresponding principles which they represent along with the teachings of the ancient Egyptian Sages relating to each. Maat philosophy was the basis of Ancient Egyptian society and government as well as the heart of Ancient Egyptian myth and spirituality. Maat is at once a goddess, a cosmic force and a living social doctrine, which promotes social harmony and thereby paves the way for spiritual evolution in all levels of society. ISBN: 1-884564-48-8 $16.95 U.S.

Guide to Creating a Kemetic Marital Agreement

35.   THE SECRET LOTUS: Poetry of Enlightenment
Discover the mystical sentiment of the Kemetic teaching as expressed through the poetry of Sebai Muata Ashby. The teaching of spiritual awakening is uniquely experienced when the poetic sensibility is present. This first volume contains the poems written between 1996 and 2003. **1-884564--16 -X $16.99**

36. The Ancient Egyptian Buddha: The Ancient Egyptian Origins of Buddhism
This book is a compilation of several sections of a larger work, a book by the name of African Origins of Civilization, Religion, Yoga Mysticism and Ethics Philosophy. It also contains some additional evidences not contained in the larger work that demonstrate the correlation between Ancient Egyptian Religion and Buddhism. This book is one of several compiled short volumes that has been compiled so as to facilitate access to specific subjects contained in the larger work which is over 680 pages long. These short and small volumes have been specifically designed to cover one subject in a brief and low cost format. This present volume, The Ancient Egyptian Buddha: The Ancient Egyptian Origins of Buddhism, formed one subject in the larger work; actually it was one chapter of the larger work. However, this volume has some new additional evidences and comparisons of Buddhist and Neterian (Ancient Egyptian) philosophies not previously discussed. It was felt that this subject needed to be discussed because even in the early 21st century, the idea persists that Buddhism originated only in India independently. Yet there is ample evidence from ancient writings and perhaps more importantly, iconographical evidences from the Ancient Egyptians and early Buddhists themselves that prove otherwise. This handy volume has been designed to be accessible to young adults and all others who would like to have an easy reference with documentation on this important subject. This is an important subject because the frame of reference with which we look at a culture depends strongly on our conceptions about its origins. in this case, if we look at the Buddhism as an Asiatic religion we would treat it and it's culture in one way. If we id as African [Ancient Egyptian] we not only would see it in a different light but we also must ascribe Africa with a glorious legacy that matches any other culture in human history and gave rise to one of the present day most important religious philosophies. We would also look at the culture and philosophies of the Ancient Egyptians as having African insights that offer us greater depth into the Buddhist philosophies. Those insights inform our knowledge about other African traditions and we can also begin to understand in a deeper way the effect of Ancient Egyptian culture on African culture and also on the Asiatic as well. We would also be able to discover the glorious and wondrous teaching of mystical philosophy that Ancient Egyptian Shetaut Neter religion offers, that is as powerful as any other mystic system of spiritual philosophy in the world today. ISBN: 1-884564-61-5 $28.95

37. The Death of American Empire: Neo-conservatism, Theocracy, Economic Imperialism, Environmental Disaster and the Collapse of Civilization

This work is a collection of essays relating to social and economic, leadership, and ethics, ecological and religious issues that are facing the world today in order to understand the course of history that has led humanity to its present condition and then arrive at positive solutions that will lead to better outcomes for all humanity. It surveys the development and decline of major empires throughout history and focuses on the creation of American Empire along with the social, political and economic policies that led to the prominence of the United States of America as a Superpower including the rise of the political control of the neo-con political philosophy including militarism and the military industrial complex in American politics and the rise of the religious right into and American Theocracy movement. This volume details, through historical and current events, the psychology behind the dominance of western culture in world politics through the "Superpower Syndrome Mandatory Conflict Complex" that drives the Superpower culture to establish itself above all others and then act hubristically to dominate world culture through legitimate influences as well as coercion, media censorship and misinformation leading to international hegemony and world conflict. This volume also details the financial policies that gave rise to American prominence in the global economy, especially after World War II, and promoted American preeminence over the world economy through Globalization as well as the environmental policies, including the oil economy, that are promoting degradation of the world ecology and contribute to the decline of America as an Empire culture. This volume finally explores the factors pointing to the decline of the American Empire economy and imperial power and what to expect in the aftermath of American prominence and how to survive the decline while at the same time promoting policies and social-economic-religious-political changes that are needed in order to promote the emergence of a beneficial and sustainable culture. **$25.95soft** 1-884564-25-9, Hard Cover **$29.95soft** 1-884564-45-3

38. The African Origins of Hatha Yoga: And its Ancient Mystical Teaching

The subject of this present volume, The Ancient Egyptian Origins of Yoga Postures, formed one subject in the larger works, African Origins of Civilization Religion, Yoga Mysticism and Ethics Philosophy and the Book Egypt and India is the section of the book African Origins of Civilization. Those works contain the collection of all correlations between Ancient Egypt and India. This volume also contains some additional information not contained in the previous work. It was felt that this subject needed to be discussed more directly, being treated in one volume, as opposed to being contained in the larger work along with other subjects, because even in the early 21st century, the idea persists that the Yoga and specifically, Yoga Postures, were invented and developed only in India. The Ancient Egyptians were peoples originally from Africa who were, in ancient times, colonists in India. Therefore it is no surprise that many Indian traditions including religious and Yogic, would be found earlier in Ancient Egypt. Yet there is ample evidence from ancient writings and perhaps more importantly, iconographical evidences from the Ancient Egyptians themselves and the Indians themselves that prove the connection between Ancient Egypt and India as well as the existence of a discipline of Yoga Postures in Ancient Egypt long before its practice in India. This handy volume has been designed to be accessible to young adults and all others who would like to have an easy reference with documentation on this important subject. This is an important subject because the frame of reference with which we look at a culture depends strongly on our conceptions about its origins. In this case, if we look at the Ancient Egyptians as Asiatic peoples we would treat them and their culture in one way. If we see them as Africans we not only see them in a different light but we also must ascribe Africa with a glorious legacy that matches any other culture in human history. We would also look at the culture and philosophies of the Ancient Egyptians as having African insights instead of Asiatic ones. Those insights inform our knowledge bout other African traditions and we can also begin to understand in a deeper way the effect of Ancient Egyptian culture on African culture and also on the Asiatic as well. When we discover the deeper and more ancient practice of the postures system in Ancient Egypt that was called "Hatha Yoga" in India, we are able to find a new and expanded understanding of the practice that constitutes a discipline of spiritual practice that informs and revitalizes the Indian practices as well as all spiritual disciplines. $19.99 ISBN 1-884564-60-7

39. The Black Ancient Egyptians

This present volume, The Black Ancient Egyptians: The Black African Ancestry of the Ancient Egyptians, formed one subject in the larger work: The African Origins of Civilization, Religion, Yoga Mysticism and Ethics Philosophy. It was felt that this subject needed to be discussed because even in the early 21st century, the idea persists that the Ancient Egyptians were peoples originally from Asia Minor who came into North-East Africa. Yet there is ample evidence from ancient writings and perhaps more importantly, iconographical evidences from the Ancient Egyptians themselves that proves otherwise. This handy volume has been designed to be accessible to young adults and all others who would like to have an easy reference with documentation on this important subject. This is an important subject because the frame of reference with which we look at a culture depends strongly on our conceptions about its origins. in this case, if we look at the Ancient Egyptians as Asiatic peoples we would treat them and their culture in one way. If we see them as Africans we not only see them in a different light but we also must ascribe Africa with a glorious legacy that matches any other culture in human history. We would also look at the culture and philosophies of the Ancient Egyptians as having African insights instead of Asiatic ones. Those insights inform our knowledge bout other African traditions and we can also begin to understand in a deeper way the effect of Ancient Egyptian culture on African culture and also on the Asiatic as well. ISBN 1-884564-21-6 $19.99

40. The Limits of Faith: The Failure of Faith-based Religions and the Solution to the Meaning of Life
Is faith belief in something without proof? And if so is there never to be any proof or discovery? If so what is the need of intellect? If faith is trust in something that is real is that reality historical, literal or metaphorical or philosophical? If knowledge is an essential element in faith why should there by so much emphasis on believing and not on understanding in the modern practice of religion? This volume is a compilation of essays related to the nature of religious faith in the context of its inception in human history as well as its meaning for religious practice and relations between religions in modern times. Faith has come to be regarded as a virtuous goal in life. However, many people have asked how can it be that an endeavor that is supposed to be dedicated to spiritual upliftment has led to more conflict in human history than any other social factor? ISBN 1884564631 SOFT COVER - $19.99, ISBN 1884564623 HARD COVER -$28.95

41. <u>Redemption of The Criminal Heart Through Kemetic Spirituality and Maat Philosophy</u>
Special book dedicated to inmates, their families and members of the Law Enforcement community. ISBN: 1-

884564-70-4
$5.00

42. COMPARATIVE MYTHOLOGY
What are Myth and Culture and what is their importance for understanding the development of societies, human evolution and the search for meaning? What is the purpose of culture and how do cultures evolve? What are the elements of a culture and how can those elements be broken down and the constituent parts of a culture understood and compared? How do cultures interact? How does enculturation occur and how do people interact with other cultures? How do the processes of acculturation and cooptation occur and what does this mean for the development of a society? How can the study of myths and the elements of culture help in understanding the meaning of life and the means to promote understanding and peace in the world of human activity? This volume is the exposition of a method for studying and comparing cultures, myths and other social aspects of a society. It is an expansion on the Cultural Category Factor Correlation method for studying and comparing myths, cultures, religions and other aspects of human culture. It was originally introduced in the year 2002. This volume contains an expanded treatment as well as several refinements along with examples of the application of the method. the apparent. I hope you enjoy these art renditions as serene reflections of the mysteries of life. ISBN: 1-884564-72-0
Book price $21.95

43. CONVERSATION WITH GOD: Revelations of the Important Questions of Life
$24.99 U.S.

This volume contains a grouping of some of the questions that have been submitted to Sebai Dr. Muata Ashby. They are efforts by many aspirants to better understand and practice the teachings of mystical spirituality. It is said that when sages are asked spiritual questions they are relaying the wisdom of God, the Goddess, the Higher Self, etc. There is a very special quality about the Q & A process that does not occur during a regular lecture session. Certain points come out that would not come out otherwise due to the nature of the process which ideally occurs after a lecture. Having been to a certain degree enlightened by a lecture certain new questions arise and the answers to these have the effect of elevating the teaching of the lecture to even higher levels. Therefore, enjoy these exchanges and may they lead you to enlightenment, peace and prosperity. Available Late Summer 2007 ISBN: 1-884564-68-2

44. MYSTIC ART PAINTINGS
(with Full Color images) This book contains a collection of the small number of paintings that I have created over the years. Some were used as early book covers and others were done simply to express certain spiritual feelings; some were created for no purpose except to express the joy of color and the feeling of relaxed freedom. All are to

elicit mystical awakening in the viewer. Writing a book on philosophy is like sculpture, the more the work is rewritten the reflections and ideas become honed and take form and become clearer and imbued with intellectual beauty. Mystic music is like meditation, a world of its own that exists about 1 inch above ground wherein the musician does not touch the ground. Mystic Graphic Art is meditation in form, color, image and reflected image which opens the door to the reality behind the apparent. I hope you enjoy these art renditions and my reflections on them as serene reflections of the mysteries of life, as visual renditions of the philosophy I have written about over the years. ISBN 1-884564-69-0 $19.95

45. **ANCIENT EGYPTIAN HIEROGLYPHS FOR BEGINNERS**

This brief guide was prepared for those inquiring about how to enter into Hieroglyphic studies on their own at home or in study groups. First of all you should know that there are a few institutions around the world which teach how to read the Hieroglyphic text but due to the nature of the study there are perhaps only a handful of people who can read fluently. It is possible for anyone with average intelligence to achieve a high level of proficiency in reading inscriptions on temples and artifacts; however, reading extensive texts is another issue entirely. However, this introduction will give you entry into those texts if assisted by dictionaries and other aids. Most Egyptologists have a basic knowledge and keep dictionaries and notes handy when it comes to dealing with more difficult texts. Medtu Neter or the Ancient Egyptian hieroglyphic language has been considered as a "Dead Language." However, dead languages have always been studied by individuals who for the most part have taught themselves through various means. This book will discuss those means and how to use them most efficiently. ISBN 1884564429 **$28.95**

46. ON THE MYSTERIES: Wisdom of An Ancient Egyptian Sage -with Foreword by Muata Ashby
This volume, On the Mysteries, by Iamblichus (Abamun) is a unique form or scripture out of the Ancient Egyptian religious tradition. It is written in a form that is not usual or which is not usually found in the remnants of Ancient Egyptian scriptures. It is in the form of teacher and disciple, much like the Eastern scriptures such as Bhagavad Gita or the Upanishads. This form of writing may not have been necessary in Ancient times, because the format of teaching in Egypt was different prior to the conquest period by the Persians, Assyrians, Greeks and later the Romans. The question and answer format can be found but such extensive discourses and corrections of misunderstandings within the context of a teacher - disciple relationship is not usual. It therefore provides extensive insights into the times when it was written and the state of practice of Ancient Egyptian and other mystery religions. This has important implications for our times because we are today, as in the Greco-Roman period, also besieged with varied religions and new age philosophies as well as social strife and war. How can we understand our times and also make sense of the forest of spiritual traditions? How can we cut through the cacophony of religious fanaticism, and ignorance as well as misconceptions about the mysteries on the other in order to discover the true purpose of religion and the secret teachings that open up the mysteries of life and the way to enlightenment and immortality? This book, which comes to us from so long ago, offers us transcendental wisdom that applied to the world two thousand years ago as well as our world today. ISBN 1-884564-64-X $25.95

47. The Ancient Egyptian Wisdom Texts -Compiled by Muata Ashby
The Ancient Egyptian Wisdom Texts are a genre of writings from the ancient culture that have survived to the present and provide a vibrant record of the practice of spiritual evolution otherwise known as religion or yoga philosophy in Ancient Egypt. The principle focus of the Wisdom Texts is the cultivation of understanding, peace, harmony, selfless service, self-control, Inner fulfillment and spiritual realization. When these factors are cultivated in human life, the virtuous qualities in a human being begin to manifest and sinfulness, ignorance and negativity diminish until a person is able to enter into higher consciousness, the coveted goal of all civilizations. It is this virtuous mode of life which opens the door to self-discovery and spiritual enlightenment. Therefore, the Wisdom Texts are important scriptures on the subject of human nature, spiritual psychology and mystical philosophy. The teachings presented in the Wisdom Texts form the foundation of religion as well as the guidelines for conducting the affairs of every area of social interaction including commerce, education, the army, marriage, and especially the legal system. These texts were sources for the famous 42 Precepts of Maat of the Pert M Heru (Book of the Dead), essential regulations of good conduct to develop virtue and purity in order to attain higher consciousness and immortality after death. ISBN1-884564-65-8 $18.95

48. THE KEMETIC TREE OF LIFE
THE KEMETIC TREE OF LIFE: Newly Revealed Ancient Egyptian Cosmology and Metaphysics for Higher Consciousness The Tree of Life is a roadmap of a journey which explains how Creation came into being and how it will end. It also explains what Creation is composed of and also what human beings are and what they are composed of. It also explains the process of Creation, how Creation develops, as well as who created Creation and where that entity may be found. It also explains how a human being may discover that entity and in so doing also discover the secrets of Creation, the meaning of life and the means to break free from the pathetic condition of human limitation and mortality in order to discover the higher realms of being by discovering the principles, the levels of existence that are beyond the simple physical and material aspects of life. This book contains color plates   **ISBN: 1-884564-74-7**
$27.95 U.S.

Guide to Creating a Kemetic Marital Agreement

49-MATRIX OF AFRICAN PROVERBS: The Ethical and Spiritual Blueprint
This volume sets forth the fundamental principles of African ethics and their practical applications for use by individuals and organizations seeking to model their ethical policies using the Traditional African values and concepts of ethical human behavior for the proper sustenance and management of society. Furthermore, this book will provide guidance as to how the Traditional African Ethics may be viewed and applied, taking into consideration the technological and social advancements in the present. This volume also presents the principles of ethical culture, and references for each to specific injunctions from Traditional African Proverbial Wisdom Teachings. These teachings are compiled from varied Pre-colonial African societies including Yoruba, Ashanti, Kemet, Malawi, Nigeria, Ethiopia, Galla, Ghana and many more. ISBN 1-884564-77-1

50- Growing Beyond Hate: Keys to Freedom from Discord, Racism, Sexism, Political Conflict, Class Warfare, Violence, and How to Achieve Peace and Enlightenment---INTRODUCTION: WHY DO WE HATE? Hatred is one of the fundamental motivating aspects of human life; the other is desire. Desire can be of a worldly nature or of a spiritual, elevating nature. Worldly desire and hatred are like two sides of the same coin in that human life is usually swaying from one to the other; but the question is why? And is there a way to satisfy the desiring or hating mind in such a way as to find peace in life? Why do human beings go to war? Why do human beings perpetrate violence against one another? And is there a way not just to understand the phenomena but to resolve the issues that plague humanity and could lead to a more harmonious society? Hatred is perhaps the greatest scourge of humanity in that it leads to misunderstanding, conflict and untold miseries of life and clashes between individuals, societies and nations. Therefore, the riddle of Hatred, that is, understanding the sources of it and how to confront, reduce and even eradicate it so as to bring forth the fulfillment in life and peace for society, should be a top priority for social scientists, spiritualists and philosophers. This book is written from the perspective of spiritual philosophy based on the mystical wisdom and sema or yoga philosophy of the Ancient Egyptians. This philosophy, originated and based in the wisdom of Shetaut Neter, the Egyptian Mysteries, and Maat, ethical way of life in society and in spirit, contains Sema-Yogic wisdom and understanding of life's predicaments that can allow a human being of any ethnic group to understand and overcome the causes of hatred, racism, sexism, violence and disharmony in life, that plague human society. ISBN: 1-884564-81-X

www.ingramcontent.com/pod-product-compliance
Lightning Source LLC
Chambersburg PA
CBHW081116080526
44587CB00021B/3626